Praise for
Why Didn't You Say That in the First Place?

"This book will help all members of an organization, from the CEO to the mail room clerk, to communicate more effectively."
—MARY ANNE FITZPATRICK, past president,
International Communication Association

"Anyone who wants to be clearly understood can't afford to miss this book. Clear communication goes straight to the bottom line."
—CLIFF FLETCHER, president and general manager,
Toronto Maple Leaf Hockey Club, and member of the
Board of Governors, National Hockey League

"Easy to read . . . easy to use . . . clear and concise . . . a practical guide that empowers the reader with techniques and strategies that guarantee true communicative understanding in all areas of one's life."
—FREDDIE GERSHON, lawyer, producer, and
chair and CEO, Music Theatre International

"Understanding the art of communication is the pursuit of many for professional and personal reasons. Dr. Heyman gives much insight into this learning process."
—SHARON J. STILLMAN, sales director,
Wauwatosa Realty

"Heyman's method of communication will result in fewer misunderstandings at work and in other contexts. Engagingly written and fun to read, this volume is a worthwhile addition to your how-to library."
—LONG ISLAND MAGAZINE

Why Didn't You Say
That in the First Place?

Why Didn't You Say That in the First Place?

How to Be Understood at Work

Richard Heyman, Ed.D.

Jossey-Bass Publishers • San Francisco

The definition of *talk* on pages 14–15 is reprinted by permission. From
Merriam-Webster's Collegiate Dictionary, Tenth Edition © 1993 by
Merriam-Webster Inc., publisher of the Merriam-Webster dictionaries.

FIRST PAPERBACK EDITION PUBLISHED IN 1997.

Substantial discounts on bulk quantities of Jossey-Bass books are
available to corporations, professional associations, and other
organizations. For details and discount information, contact the
special sales department at Jossey-Bass Inc., Publishers
(415) 433–1740; Fax (800) 605-2665.

For sales outside the United States, please contact your local Simon &
Schuster International office.

Jossey-Bass Web address: http://www.josseybass.com

 Manufactured in the United States of America on Lyons Falls Turin
Book. This paper is acid-free and 100 percent totally chlorine-free.

Library of Congress Cataloging-in-Publication Data

Heyman, Richard
    Why didn't you say that in the first place? : how to be understood
at work / Richard Heyman. — 1st ed.
       p. cm — (The Jossey-Bass management series)
    Includes bibliographical references and index.
    ISBN 1-55542-653-0
    ISBN 0-7879-0344-2 (paperback)
    1. Communication in organizations.   2. Communication in
personnel management.   3. Interpersonal communication.   I. Title.
II. Series.
HD30.3.H49   1994
650.1´3—dc20   93-48663

FIRST EDITION
HB Printing   10 9 8 7 6 5 4 3 2
PB Printing   10 9 8 7 6 5 4 3 2 1

The Jossey-Bass Business & Management Series

Contents

Preface

"Why didn't you say that in the first place?" Is this a question that you hear yourself asking or that you hear asked of you? Here is a book that explains why misunderstandings are normal and what you can do to improve your chances of being understood as you would like to be. It is the perfect book for those who find misunderstanding a common and frustrating experience and want to know what to do about it.

Why I Wrote This Book

I wrote this book to give you the power to make sure that everyone knows what you mean by what you say or write. Studies of the way we communicate, as well as our own experience, tell us that others will often misunderstand what we say or write. When we understand why misunderstanding happens so regularly, we can use ordinary language to ensure understanding in a wide variety of situations and greatly reduce the chances of misunderstanding. Once we know how to do this, the success or failure of our communication depends largely on us. It is our responsibility and no one else's. We make the difference.

Using research in the field of ethnomethodology and the analysis of everyday talk, I show you a new way of understanding how we make sense of each other's language. The research explains why misunderstanding is a common experience. It's not simply the result of people being unable to express themselves clearly or not knowing what they should know. Misunderstanding occurs naturally because all our understanding of language depends on our interpretation of language in context. We must decide, however, what that context is. We can communicate clearly when we share a context for understanding. When we don't, misunderstanding results. The solution lies in using the knowledge and techniques of what I call *strategic talk* to create a shared context.

You don't have to learn a new language to use strategic talk. You can use your normal, everyday talk in a systematic way based on your new knowledge of misunderstanding.

Why This Book Is Needed

We all experience misunderstanding in the workplace. It doesn't matter how clearly we think we speak or write—others still misunderstand us, and misunderstandings cost us and our organizations time and money. The problem we all face is knowing why misunderstanding happens and how to prevent it. If we can solve that problem, we can help ourselves and our organizations.

This book shows, for the first time, how to use the insights of ethnomethodology to help people in organizations learn about the methods available to make sense of each other's ideas through talk. Ethnomethodologists study talk and action in people's ordinary, everyday lives using films, audiotapes, and videotapes to observe and analyze the methods that people use in interactions. They don't try to guess what is going on in people's minds, but show how people understand and misunderstand each other by looking at what the people involved in the interaction can all see and hear.

Why Didn't You Say That in the First Place? uses a nonpsychological approach to studying communication, offering a new understanding of misunderstanding in organizations. You can use this new awareness and its solutions alongside other approaches to solving your communication problems. The other approaches generally rely on social psychological or sociolinguistic research and provide a more familiar overview of communication problems.

Who Should Read This Book?

If you want people to understand you when you talk and you want to understand them, this book is for you. It can help make your everyday work life more productive and more profitable, by making you more attuned to the way people make sense of what you say. Whether you are an executive, a manager, a secretary, a salesperson, a file clerk, a consultant, a waiter or waitress, a bank teller, a mechanic, an engineer, a builder, a plumber, an electrician, or a carpenter, reading this book can help you. Whether you work in finance, retail, wholesale, manufacturing, shipping, service, advertising, tourism, food services, construction, entertainment, media, government, sports, or social services, this book will offer you new ways to ensure understanding. If you are a consultant in organizational communication and unfamiliar with the insights of ethnomethodology, you will find some interesting ideas about language use and the issues surrounding it that you can adapt in your work. Teachers, parents, and students can also use the methods described here. No matter what your position, this book will save you time and money and make your work relationships easier.

Overview of the Contents

I have grouped the eight chapters of the book into three parts, each of which examines a different aspect of misunderstanding. Part One (the first two chapters) shows how the root causes of misunderstanding lie in our language. Chapter One sets the stage by describing how misunderstanding creates problems for us all and how it can create small or large costs within our organizations. I discuss ethnomethodological research, showing that language is naturally vague and ambiguous and that understanding the indexical and reflexive nature of language can open ways to make our talk more precise.

Chapter Two explains how talk and context are the two basic ingredients for understanding, and it discusses how we understand each other by taking turns as speakers and listeners. We see that strategic talk works to prevent misunderstanding by using normal patterns of speech in a special, systematic way.

Part Two (Chapters Three, Four, and Five) demonstrates how to use your new comprehension of misunderstanding to ensure understanding in your organizational life. Chapter Three looks carefully at the language of work and ways to use strategic talk in real-life situations to ensure understanding.

Chapter Four explains why written language is even more ambiguous and confusing than talk and why important written communication needs follow-up discussion. I provide specific strategies for ensuring that our written words get understood the way we intended.

Chapter Five shows how you can use strategic talk to communicate well with people who are different from you. This means forgetting about stereotypes and realizing that the problem of understanding is universal. We must explicitly create a shared context for understanding in our interactions.

Part Three (Chapters Six, Seven, and Eight) looks at how through strategic talk an organization can create systems that foster clear communication. Chapter Six examines the link between successful leadership and clear communication. It offers tools for building a culture that encourages people to say without fear, "I don't understand. Can you make that a bit clearer?" Such a culture must be built on a foundation of knowledge about both the root cause of and the cure for misunderstanding.

Chapter Seven shows how to establish systems in your organization to ensure clear communication in important areas. The systems are modeled on those used by high-reliability organizations, in which operational failure can spell disaster. Using these systems in combination with strategic talk can give you a significant competitive advantage.

Chapter Eight shows that organizations that take talk seriously create a new accountability. Once you understand that misunderstanding is normal and how strategic talk can remedy it, then you are accountable for your own misunderstanding. Once you know how to clarify talk in critical situations, lack of understanding can no longer be used as an excuse for doing work wrong. Clear communication must be tackled anew in each situation.

Scope of the Book

I did not include discussion of certain areas of life that have a bearing on how we talk to one another because I have no new insights about them. For example, we each have personal agendas, fears, and desires that affect how and what we say to people and how they understand us. In this book, I concentrate on the public face of communication, that which is hearable. I have tried to stay out of people's minds, even though we all know that our private thoughts do make a difference. I have not examined at any length people's hidden motives for saying what they say, since those motives cannot be known in the absence of words or actions. I also have not explicitly discussed body language or intonation and the ways they affect meaning; many excellent books on these subjects are already available. From the perspective taken here, body language and intonation are part of the context for understanding, and our job in making sense of the spoken word is to decide on their meaning and importance.

My hope is that, in spite of these intentional omissions, once you have read *Why Didn't You Say That in the First Place?* you will have an enriched understanding of the problems that we all face in trying to make sense of what the people we work with are saying. You will have the skills to help solve those problems using the power of talk, and the knowledge and skills you will acquire can make you a more compassionate, flexible, creative, innovative, understanding, and successful person.

Acknowledgments

Every author owes a debt of gratitude to more people than can possibly be acknowledged in the space permitted. Nevertheless, let me try.

For inspiration, knowledge, suggestions, and the good sense not always to tell me the truth about my book in its early stages, I would like to thank Lynn Bosetti, Reid Campbell, Frederic Gershon, Judith Gingrich, David Glassman, Peter Graves, Janet McFadden, Allan Markin, Robert Schmor, William Taylor, David Thomas, and Michael Vanry.

For showing interest in my rough ideas, for having a great sense of humor, for having years of experience and success in publishing, for patiently giving me the encouragement, advice, and tools to make my ideas useful, understandable, and marketable, I thank my agent, Michael Snell, president of Michael Snell Literary Agency.

For taking my manuscript and turning it into a book that people will find interesting, useful, and easy to read, I thank my editor, Sarah Polster, her assistant, Barbara Hill, and my copyeditor, Laura Larson. To my developmental editor, Janet Hunter, I can say only that without her insights, suggestions, and organizational and editorial skill, many parts of the book would still be more idea than substance.

My debt to Harold Garfinkel goes beyond anything I can say. Through his genius I came to a new understanding of the way we make sense of each other's words. My goal has been to make these insights available to others. I also thank the University of Calgary Killam Resident Fellowship Program for its support of this project.

Finally I thank my family, both nearby and faraway, for their diplomatic comments and tongue-biting silences at every stage in the development and writing of *Why Didn't You Say That.* . . . I know that if the book is successful, my compulsive-obsessive behavior of the past three years will be forgiven.

Calgary, Alberta   RICHARD HEYMAN
June 1994

The Author

RICHARD HEYMAN is a professor at the University of Calgary, where he teaches courses in conversation analysis and ethnomethodology. Born and raised in New York City, he holds a B.A. degree in English from Cornell University, a postgraduate diploma in English studies from the University of Edinburgh, an M.A. degree in social sciences and education from Columbia University, a certificate in African studies from Columbia University, and an Ed.D. degree from Columbia University. He has been a Ford Foundation Fellow and a visiting fellow at Wolfson College, Cambridge University. Currently, he is director of the Discourse Analysis Research Group, an international network of people who study language use in everyday life. He is an internationally recognized scholar who has published more than thirty articles and chapters in scholarly journals and books. He has more than fifteen years' experience in business and is president of Richard Heyman Associates, a communications consulting company that has worked with both small and large businesses as well as social welfare and educational agencies.

Part One

Why Nobody
Understands You

Chapter One

For Your Ears Only:
Why Misunderstanding Is Normal

The corporation's most powerful marketing push in many years has been launched throughout the United States and Canada. Deborah, vice president for marketing, and William, marketing manager for North America, are talking about the initiative over drinks, trying to decide whether their efforts will be successful enough to repair the damage that competition has done to sales over the past five years.

William: We seem to be moving straight and steady.

Deborah: And gaining momentum, according to your latest figures.

William: I think we can really win with this one as long as we stick to our plan.

Deborah: Except that we've had some losers over the past few years.

William: I'm sure we've got a winner here.

Deborah: I hope you're right, or I'm going to be facing a lot of angry shareholders.

William: What's that supposed to mean?

Deborah: Lately you seem to be unwilling to admit your mistakes. Have you noticed that?

William: Come on, now, Deborah.

Deborah: You do, William. You really do.

William: I don't.

Deborah: See?

William: See what?

Deborah: There you go again.

William: What are you playing at, Deborah? I can disagree with you when I know I'm right.

Deborah: But we have lost some market share recently.

William: I agree.

Deborah: Then why did you say we haven't?

William: What? That's what I said. I said that this plan can help us get back what we lost.

Deborah: If you had really said that, I would have agreed with you.

Do you hear yourself in this conversation? How often have you argued with someone about what you did or didn't say? Virtually everyone has experienced this kind of misunderstanding at work. But imagine what your organization would be like if everyone in it understood each other all the time. It would certainly be a different kind of place to work. Jobs would be done right the first time. Orders and deliveries would be accurate and on time. There would be no arguments with customers, clients, or associates about who said what and who meant what. We wouldn't have to second-guess our bosses or read their minds. Can we create such an organization? The answer is yes, within the limits of what our language will allow.

This book can help you minimize misunderstanding. To be a good communicator, you must learn to understand misunderstanding. With that knowledge, you can take steps to ensure clear communication. You can learn how to use ordinary, everyday language to create a shared context for understanding to make communication as clear as it can possibly be. The secret is to use your language systematically, knowing when to use it and why.

Research has shown that we can take some straightforward, useful, and practical steps to ensure clear communication; this book will show you what those steps are. In the process, you will learn why misunderstanding happens so often in spite of our efforts to prevent it. This knowledge is not difficult but will significantly change your understanding of how we make sense of language. Your new understanding of misunderstanding will, in itself, be a valuable tool to change how you interact with people inside and outside your organization. Some clear, obvious ways of talking follow from this particular view of misunderstanding. By using them, you will maximize the chances that you and your associates will understand each other, and you will minimize the chances of misunderstanding. Learning to overcome misunderstanding will take courage and training, even though the practices themselves are techniques and ways of talking that we already use every day. With a full understanding of these ideas and some practice, you can make your organization a place where misunderstanding is the exception rather than the rule.

Misunderstanding Costs Time and Money

To justify the effort necessary to learn and act with newfound knowledge, we need to understand how misunderstanding costs all organizations time and money. Learning how to avoid misunderstanding—and teaching others to avoid it—goes right to the bottom line. Consider these points:

- When jobs have to be done a second or third time because of misunderstandings, the company wastes time and money.
- Misunderstandings can eat up valuable time and often cause projects to go over budget.
- When people misunderstand the point of important meetings, their misunderstandings cost time and money.
- Employees who misunderstand their job responsibilities waste their time and the company's money.
- Misunderstanding clients' wishes and needs costs time and money.

- Misunderstanding important letters, memos, reports, and other written material costs time and money.
- If your associates or employees misunderstand your ideas, time and money can be lost.
- Misunderstandings that cause operational failure or cause a shutdown cost time and money.
- Misunderstandings that require court settlements of contract disputes cost time and money.
- Misunderstandings that lead to claims of sexual harassment cost time and money.
- Misunderstandings that arise because people don't know how to talk to people of different backgrounds can waste a lot of time and money.

Even with all the potential costs of misunderstanding, few people realize that misunderstanding is a normal problem in nearly every organization, and for some fundamental reasons. In fact, this realization can come as a big surprise.

Don, a trained engineer and a manager for the subsidiary of a multinational oil company, and I were talking about Don's work. We got onto the topic of misunderstanding, and he told me about some very frustrating problems he had with his employees, especially new engineers.

They'd come to him for their assignments, and he'd tell them carefully what he wanted them to do. They'd say, "Yes, sir" and go off to do the work. About a week later, they'd come back to show him what they had done. All too often they'd gotten it wrong and hadn't done the work the way Don wanted. He had to sit down and carefully go through with them again exactly what he wanted done, even though he thought he'd made it perfectly clear the first time. He told me that the engineers were people who had been trained at the finest colleges and who really should have known their work.

The second time through, these new people might say, "Oh! So you wanted me to do it that way. Now I understand. Sorry for the mistake." And off they went to do it again. Even if they still didn't get it perfectly right, it was better than the first time. According to Don, none of these people had ever said they didn't understand what he was saying. Whether they didn't recognize that they didn't understand Don's wishes or did and were afraid to admit it, the result was the same.

Misunderstanding Is Normal

Like Don, people are often surprised when others misunderstand them. People take it for granted that others will understand them and if they don't, they believe it's because they, or the others, are deficient in some way. Because Don's employees assumed that the meaning of talk was normally clear as long as people knew their jobs and expressed themselves properly, his employees were in a double bind. If they said they didn't understand Don, it meant that they were incompetent, because they should have known what he wanted. Worse still, saying they didn't understand could mean that their new boss was incompetent for not having made his directions more clear. No wonder they always just smiled and went off to try to do the best job they could.

From my perspective, the problem wasn't caused by Don not knowing how to express himself clearly or by his employees not knowing their jobs. The problem was that neither Don nor his employees understood that misunderstanding is normal—and what to do to correct it.

Our talk has the power to create and shape our world by telling others in our organization how we see it and how we want it to be, according to our own wishes, desires, and needs. We hope others understand us; however, they often misunderstand us. Misunderstanding destroys the power of talk. It causes things to go wrong, to go in ways we didn't want them to go at all. We end up with arguments, mistakes, missed meetings, lost sales, bad feelings, and countless other problems. The consequences can be annoying, or even harmful, for us and for our organizations. It's a frustrating and persistent experience, and we usually blame ourselves or others for it happening.

But there's another way to understand the cause and cure for most misunderstanding: the basic nature of language itself causes misunderstanding. Knowing this, we can use that same language to ensure that people will normally understand us. Using certain parts of our normal, everyday talk in a systematic way will give us the power to communicate clearly and avoid misunderstanding insofar as that is humanly possible.

Misunderstanding Is Everyone's Problem

Because misunderstanding can affect how well we do our jobs, misunderstanding is our personal problem. Making sure that we understand each other is our responsibility. Knowing what causes most misunderstanding and how to prevent it will give us new power to do the best job we can for ourselves and for our organizations.

There's no question about the importance of clear communication and the difficulty in finding it. In fact, communication often appears at the top of lists of areas that need improvement in organizations. Margot Gibb-Clark reports that in a survey of executives from two hundred of the thousand largest U.S. companies, 74 percent said writing skills, oral communication skills, and people skills were the hardest to find in job candidates. The survey was done for Robert Half International Inc., a recruiting firm, whose chairperson said, "Good communicators are in high demand because they create more efficient and effective teams." In a recent issue of *Fortune*, Faye Rice echoes an unnamed consultant who estimates that only 10 percent of CEOs "are effective communicators, who talk candidly with employees, encouraging them to contribute ideas." Clearly, we must take steps to improve communication.

How Talk Makes Sense

I am often asked about my line of work. When I explain that I am a professor who teaches conversation analysis, people usually say something like "How am I doing?" or "What can you tell me about myself?" or "Can you tell where people are from and all that?"

To most people, conversation analysis sounds like what Professor Henry Higgins did with Eliza Doolittle in My Fair Lady to change her from a Cockney-speaking flower girl into a proper lady with an upper-class English accent. But I don't do that. I study how people use ordinary language to make sense of each other in everyday conversation. To do this, I use a model of communication that comes out of research done since 1959 in an area of study called ethnomethodology. In simple terms this means:

ethno/method/ology = people / method / the study of
The study of people's methods for making sense of each other

When he was a student at Harvard, the eminent sociologist Harold Garfinkel realized that social scientists rarely studied how ordinary people, talking, working, and just living their everyday lives, managed to make sense of each other in order to accomplish simple and complex projects together. He coined the term ethnomethodology to describe his study of people's everyday lives and communication with others. He wanted to describe the methods that we use to make our social world an accountable, rational, factual, real, reportable, storyable, describable, shared world.

Ethnomethodology gives us a model built on two observable and fundamental features of language: indexicality (the meaning of language depends on the context) and reflexivity (the context of language depends on the meaning). In this view of language, all words have multiple meanings. These meanings are narrowed down by the context in which the words are used. The word that best illustrates this idea is the pronoun it. If you say to an associate, "Have you done it yet?" the word it has meaning only in the context that you and your associate can provide. It may mean a report, a letter, moving a computer, or making a phone call. What is true of the way the word it has meaning is equally true of all words in our language. Until we have a context for their meaning, all words and combinations of words, such as phrases and sentences, are ambiguous. We call this feature of language its indexicality because it refers to the embeddedness of words as we find them in the context of their use.

However, context doesn't give us a simple solution to the problem of meaning because context itself is indexical. In other words, context does not automatically exist as some clear, unambiguous framework for meaning because the factors that make up a context—like the speaker, the situation, the place, the time, the biographies of the people present—are themselves ambiguous. Just like the words they're giving meaning to, they also derive their meaning from the context in which they're found. We have to decide which identities, memberships, and other features about the person, situation, talk, place, time, and so on, are important or relevant to understanding the meaning of what's being said. We have to interpret the meaning of the situation. The meaning depends on our interpretation, which is based on the context; at the same time, the context is also an interpretation. Meaning and context each provide the grounds for the other. This seems a bit convoluted at first glance. Let's look at a real-world example.

When we're in a business meeting, what makes it a business meeting? What makes it different from a casual conversation, or a lecture, or a hobby group, or a parent-teacher meeting? It isn't the physical space. We can have a business meeting anywhere: in a bar, a plane, a hotel suite, an office, or even an elevator. It isn't the people. Presumably we could have a business meeting with anyone as long as they agree to have one with us. The kind of talk we use makes it a business meeting. We say things like "Mary, let's discuss that contract. I think we might have to make some changes" and "Sure, Bev. I've been thinking about it a lot and I agree it needs more work."

But why do we use that kind of talk? Because it's a business meeting. And why is it a business meeting? Because of the talk. The talk provides meaning for the context, and the context provides meaning for the talk. By talking business, we are involved in creating the reality in which talking business is possible. In ethnomethodology, we call this feature of language its *reflexivity*. Language's reflexivity explains why we can truly say that we, as human beings, jointly create the social world in which we live.

The indexicality and reflexivity of language explain the problem of misunderstanding. Because words take their meaning from the context in which they're used, misunderstanding happens when the speaker creates one context for understanding while the listener creates a different one. In other words, because the context isn't automatically there, because it comes from each one of us making our own interpretation, we can never completely eliminate the possibility of misunderstanding. But there is a solution for all practical purposes. The solution comes from having the knowledge and strategies to anticipate and repair misunderstanding by creating a shared context for understanding.

We may think that language is normally clear and precise as long as we speak clearly and listen carefully. How then can intelligent and competent people misunderstand simple directions, rules, job assignments, or suggestions? To understand this, we must realize that talk is routinely vague and ambiguous. But if our talk is really so vague and ambiguous, why doesn't our everyday talk with others cause us endless problems? After all, people don't constantly say, "I'm sorry, but I don't understand exactly what you're saying. Would you mind being more precise?" If we're being vague and ambiguous, why don't people tell us? People don't ask for clarification all the time, as Don's employees demonstrated, because saying that they don't understand can be very embarrassing. People are afraid others may think them dumb, or inattentive, or incompetent. Those who believe that most talk should be clear if the language is used properly think that admitting misunderstanding reflects badly on the speaker or the listener.

Ethnomethodology shows that talk is necessarily indexical and reflexive because these features allow us to make sense of people in our everyday lives without requiring that we know everything they know. This makes our social lives possible. If all words needed precise meaning and context for any understanding to take place, communication would be unimaginable because we could never hope to have a big enough vocabulary or enough background knowledge to talk to most other people. The two aspects of talk that create most misunderstanding also allow us to have a social world where we can talk to and make sense of people.

Harold Garfinkel conducted some informal experiments to show what happens when we ask people to say exactly what they mean. He called these "breaching" experiments. They were designed to try to destroy our common-sense reality by creating situations in which our normal expectations about how we talk to one another are breached. At the same time they showed what those expectations are by reporting what we say and do in these situations. He had people volunteer as experimenters to start a conversation with someone they knew and ask for clarification of statements that would normally be unquestioned. He wanted to show how much we take it for granted that others will understand us and how much we depend on them to fill in what we don't say ourselves. In almost every case the conversation had the following pattern:

Subject: How are you?

Experimenter: How am I in regard to what? My health, my finances, my work, my peace of mind . . . ?

Subject (red in the face and suddenly out of control): Look, I was just trying to be polite. Frankly, I don't give a damn how you are.

Here is another example, based on my students' experiments:

Subject: Hi, Mary. How is the work going?

Experimenter: What do you mean, "How is it going?" Do you mean mentally or financially?

Subject: I mean "How is it going?" What's the matter with you?

Experimenter: Nothing. Could you just explain a little clearer what you want to know?

Subject: Skip it. How is that new project coming?

Experimenter: What do you mean, "How is it coming?"

Subject: You know what I mean.

Experimenter: I really don't.

Subject: What's the matter with you? Are you sick?

These exchanges teach us some important lessons about how we communicate with each other:

- People expect us to make sense of what they say even when they are not precise. They take it for granted that we will understand them and depend on us to fill in what they haven't said themselves. Ethnomethodologists call this expectation that we will fill in what hasn't been explicitly and precisely said the *et cetera principle*. People don't expect to be asked what they mean, even if those who hear them don't precisely understand.

- People trust us to fill in the correct meaning. If we don't, we are violating that trust and raising serious questions about our membership in the group of people who ought to understand without asking questions. Our questioning can reflect badly on us because it raises questions about what we know and what we ought to know.

- When we ask people to be more precise about what they're saying, they often get annoyed and defensive. This reaction is in part because our questions make it appear as though the people talking are not expressing themselves clearly, even though they assumed they were. In this sense, our questions can be perceived as reflecting badly on the speakers.

These aspects of communication have important consequences for our lives in organizations. We can't ask everyone to say exactly what they mean all the time. If we did, they'd likely stop talking to us because we're violating their trust in us to fill in the correct meaning for what they say. Happily, we don't have to seek precise communication all the time because much of what we say doesn't need to be precise. We can usually fill in what we have to and assume that it's right. As long as our understanding isn't put to some test, misunderstanding never becomes an issue. We can also imagine situations in which misunderstanding is a positive occurrence because it leads to serendipitous solutions to problems that might otherwise have been missed. But situations at work arise when it's critical that we understand precisely what someone means. For example, when someone asks us to do a job, we have to understand what the job entails and how to get it done correctly and on time. In those cases we have to know what to do to avoid misunderstanding. The indexicality and reflexivity of language can make that problematic.

All Words Have Many Possible Meanings

The meaning of words isn't a simple equation:

one word = one meaning

talk   = to say things with words

Instead, it looks more like this:

one word = a very large number of possible meanings, some
              of which are at complete odds with one another

talk   = (v) to deliver or express in speech: utter; to make
              the subject of conversation or discourse: discuss;
              to influence, affect, or cause by talking; to use (a
              language) for conversing or communicating:
              speak; to express or exchange ideas by means of
              spoken words; to convey information or commu-
              nicate in any way (as with signs or sounds); to use
              speech: speak; to speak idly: prate; gossip; to
              reveal secret or confidential information; to give
              a talk: lecture; to answer impertinently; to voice
              rational, logical, or sensible thoughts; to voice
              irrational, illogical, or erroneous ideas; to speak

frankly or bluntly. (n) the act or an instance of talking: speech; a way of speaking: language; pointless or fruitless discussion: verbiage; a formal discussion, negotiation, or exchange of views; mention, report; rumor, gossip; the topic of interested comment, conversation, or gossip; address, lecture; written analysis or discussion presented in an informal or conversational manner; communicative sounds or signs resembling or functioning as talk.

Each one of these definitions would give a different meaning to any utterance in which the word *talk* was used. Unless the speaker tells us explicitly which definition she or he intends, we must work it out from the context of the talk. But what is the correct context? Take the following as an example:

Georgina: John, I'd like you to talk to the computer people this afternoon. They're coming over about the new system.

Can you tell what meaning of "talk" John is supposed to fill in? You can't, can you? At least not without knowing more about the context. Is John supposed to yell at the computer people, explain something to them, or thank them? Or perhaps he is to tell them no, or tell them yes, or even ask them some questions. Will John know? If Georgina doesn't make it more explicit, then John has to hope he understands her meaning. There's presumably much shared experience that he can draw on, but John still has to guess Georgina's intentions. He may guess right or he may guess wrong. Or he may say, "Georgina, what exactly do you want me to discuss?" Questions such as this are ways to help make people's talk understandable.

Reading Minds and Misunderstanding

People trust us to fill in the correct meaning of what they say even when they don't say it clearly or precisely. They assume we already have enough background knowledge to understand much more than what they actually say. This creates two problems for us. First, it means that we have to interpret their actual words correctly. Second, we have to interpret accurately all the things that they have left unsaid. In other words, we have to be able to read their minds. No wonder misunderstanding is normal.

You may know your longtime business associates well and think that you can read their minds. If you can, then the problem of misunderstanding between you will never arise because you can know their thoughts, motives, intentions, and meaning directly, without having to understand their talk. But how much would you be willing to risk on that? Even if you've worked together for a long time and often seem to be able to tell what the other is thinking, it's a chancy way of communicating. And when it doesn't work, you wind up hearing something like "I can't believe you didn't know what I meant. How many years have we been together? Surely I don't have to spell out everything for you."

Remedies to the Problem of Misunderstanding That Require Us to Read Other People's Minds Are No Remedies at All!

Ethnomethodology examines how people make sense of each other by focusing on their talk in context. It assumes that we can't take a shortcut to understanding by reading minds. With what consistency can you tell exactly what people were thinking, what motivated them, what kind of mental processes their talk represented, and therefore, why they said what they said, what it means, and what you're supposed to do as a result? In real life most of us can't read minds well enough to depend on doing it as a usual means of doing business.

Of course, we're always trying to figure out what people are thinking. I'm not suggesting that we stop trying. We do have to start talking to people, and that involves some guessing at what they already know and what their context for understanding might be. However, even though we can't avoid some attempt at this, expecting people to read minds is not the way to remedy misunderstanding in organizations. A better way lies in knowing how talk works.

Understanding Talk Requires Shared Context

Context—the baseline data, the foundation of our experience of the world—gives meaning to all that we say or write. It may be our name, birthplace, family, education, beliefs, loyalties, motives, desires, goals, prejudices, knowledge, skills, abilities, resentments, organization, town, state, country, color, sex, body positioning, facial expressions, gestures, intonation, and much more. The context we actually use to understand someone's talk may be all of these factors, a few of them, or none of them. The context forms our interpretation of the factors that we use to understand at that moment in time; it is not fixed forever.

Since we provide the context for meaning, we can make sense of almost anything. That's the beauty of the way language works. We simply fill in the context we think is correct in order to give meaning to the talk. We human beings are really talented at making sense of the strangest things, as well as the most familiar. We can talk to people we've never met before concerning topics about which we know very little, or nothing, and still make sense of the talk.

But that's also the danger. We can make sense of the talk in the wrong way. Because context always comes from us, our context, and therefore our understanding, may be different from the one the speaker intends us to have. Thus, our interpretations can be at the root of our misunderstanding.

In making sense of talk, we create the context when we decide what fits. You might think of context as the who, what, where, when, why, and how of any situation. In fact, although doing so is a bit of an oversimplification, we often—and even unconsciously—rely on questions such as the following to frame our context:

- Who's talking?
- What are they talking about? What are the words they're using? What might their personal interests be? What might they think my interests are?
- Where are we talking?

- When is the conversation taking place? When is an answer expected?
- Why are they saying what they're saying?
- How does what they're saying relate to other things I know about them?

These might look like simple questions, but they're not necessarily easy to answer with any accuracy.

People's context can lead to quite different descriptions of an apparently factual event. Ethnomethodologists will tell you that a literal description is impossible because all description is an interpretation. It's a choice of whom to describe, what to describe, where and when to describe, for what purpose to describe (the why), and how to describe. This reinforces the notion that we actively create our social world through our accounts of it based on the context we provide for understanding. In order to understand each other, we have to make sure that we understand and share the context for interpreting these accounts.

What Happens When Contexts Aren't Shared?

The following story shows how easy it is for people to use different contexts for understanding the same words. One day as David was walking down the hall, his boss called him into her office and said, "David, what do you think of affirmative action?" David's immediate response was "It certainly hasn't hurt our company. Especially since we depend on government contracts for much of our work." Looking serious, his boss then responded, "Yes, I know, but I was thinking of affirmative action with respect to my son who is applying to law school this year. He's afraid that he might not get in unless he scores really high on the law aptitude test because so many women and minority groups are applying."

David's response reflects the context he thought was appropriate. His context included being at work and in conversation with his boss, hearing the question as a business question, relating to a government program, and the politics of doing business. But this wasn't the context his boss was using. She was asking a personal question and speaking to David as a man, or a parent, or both. She was looking for any one of a number of different kinds of answers: practical, experiential, ethical, or moral, for example. Her context seems to include a parent's concern for her child, the reverse discrimination she perceives in government policy, and how her child might be put at a disadvantage.

Here's another example of what happens when contexts for meaning aren't shared. Lucy Suchman, an anthropologist working for Xerox Corporation, has researched problems of misunderstanding in the workplace that arise when people use photocopying machines. Suchman studied the design of a self-instructional photocopying machine that was supposed to allow first-time users to use the machine quickly and efficiently to complete their photocopying jobs. The design was important to Xerox because ease of use is an important sales feature for these machines.

Observations of people using an earlier version of the machine, which had only written instructions, showed that the machine was too complicated to be used by a novice with no training. People had lots of problems in reading the written instructions and then performing the appropriate action to get their copies. The new machine had a computer-based system, designed to solve this problem. The machine displayed an instruction for action, the user did the action, the machine then displayed the next instruction, and so on until the photocopying job was done. The user just had to make his or her actions match the words on the display.

As a test of this system, people were videotaped using the machine in pairs and talking to each other as they tried to follow the instructions the machine provided. Examination of the videotape revealed that users had trouble understanding the instructions the machine displayed. The users made mistakes and were sometimes unable to photocopy their material. The principal problem was found to lie in the answers the machine gave to the user's question "What do I do next?"

The computer-based help system was designed using a model that assumed that words are clear and unambiguous. Using this model the designer created a step-by-step set of instructions for the machine to display to the users. The words in the machine's messages were supposed to have just one meaning that users would all know and understand. Unfortunately, users often thought the machine's message meant one thing when it really meant something else.

In one instance, a user was trying to make copies of a book. She had successfully completed steps 0 and 1. When the machine displayed the message for step 2, "Slide the document cover left over your original until it latches," the user mistakenly closed the entire "Bound Document Aid" instead. The machine responded with the message for step 1 again. But the user wanted to move to the next instruction so she selected "Change Task Description?" The machine then displayed step 0. The user said she had already done that and didn't want to do it again; she then selected "Help." But the machine's sensor said she was at step 0 and gave her help for that, whereas she wanted help in knowing why the machine had gone back to step 0 display in the first place.

The user and machine misunderstood each other because each had a different sense of what the context was and what the words of the message meant in that context. People misunderstand each other for the same reason. The meaning of language is intimately tied to how we understand context.

Deep Differences in Context

Problems of misunderstanding arise when we expect others to read our minds in order to know what we want them to do. Another problem area that is similar stems from the wide range of personal differences that we bring to our jobs. These include differences in our feelings, desires, motivations, fears, and ambitions; our values and valuing; our own self-images; and our likes and dislikes toward our jobs, organizations, associates, clients, customers, and competition. How then can we relate to and work with others in the organization who are different from us in ways that would appear to make clear communication and good working relationships virtually impossible?

For example, you may be a person who values ideas, exciting new visions, creativity, and the big picture, and you're working on a project with someone whose approach to new tasks is linear, detailed, cautious, and conservative. Or perhaps you relate to your job and your colleagues in an emotional way, valuing them as individuals whom you have known for varying periods of time, and your associate thinks of people as workers who are no more valuable than their performance on their last project. Such deep differences in the context of how we relate to people in the organization can create problems of understanding that seem unresolvable. We may be using the same language, even the same words, but since we're on different wavelengths, the words take on totally different meanings.

Deep differences undoubtedly exist between people. The job of explaining why and how they exist, their source, how they change, and how they show themselves must be left to the appropriate experts. The analysis of misunderstanding presented in this book makes no claim to explaining what goes on inside people's minds. Instead, we can use strategic talk to bring these differences to light, make them more apparent, and make our different contexts for understanding explicit. Strategic talk is a tool to work with what we have in the interaction: the background knowledge, all the other appropriate contextual particulars, and the talk itself.

In the moment of the talk and interaction, deep differences may surface. We therefore have to interpret others' talk and action and figure out what to say and do next. Whatever the true source or cause of problems in the interaction, we have to work with our interpretation of it and take our turn. We might choose to walk away, get someone to replace us or the other person, ask someone to mediate the problem, get expert advice, change jobs, or take other steps that we think can solve the problem in some way. Or we could use strategic talk to work at creating shared context by pointing out what we don't share and making explicit what we need to share. With this tactic, we try to work out the problem for all practical purposes and forget about trying to change people at the deepest level of their personality. Strategic talk treats the symptoms, not the disease, by trying to create a workable shared context for understanding in the interaction. If there is misunderstanding, for whatever reason, strategic talk makes it visible.

Summary

Misunderstanding creates problems for all of us in the workplace. The test for understanding is success, a job done with no trouble. When we don't understand each other, work doesn't get done right. Time and money are wasted. Once we understand why misunderstanding is normal and how it's caused by the nature of language itself more than by speakers' or writers' brains, psyches, or personalities, we can remedy misunderstanding using the power of common, everyday talk in a skillful, thoughtful way.

Thanks to the inherent vagueness and ambiguity of language, misunderstanding is normal. This doesn't mean that it is good or that it happens all the time, just that it's fairly common. We may think the cause of the problem is that people don't say what they mean. However, if we try to get people to say precisely what they mean in ordinary conversation, they're likely to think there is something wrong with us. They trust us to know what they mean and to fill in all the blanks they left unsaid but that are important to our understanding them.

Ethnomethodology shows us that talk is indexical, in that the meaning of language depends on the context in which it's used, and reflexive, since the context depends on the meaning of language. The problem of misunderstanding comes from the fact that the context for understanding each other isn't automatically there. We are each responsible for creating our own context for understanding. When our context differs from the one the speaker intends, we misunderstand each other.

When we know the strengths and limitations of talk, we can use that knowledge to anticipate and fix the problem. Understanding the interpretive nature of language gives us the power to create misunderstanding when we want to (knowing that it can sometimes serendipitously lead to new ideas and solutions to problems) and to prevent it when we want to. The consequences of misunderstanding, whether trivial, catastrophic, or somewhere in between, can create problems for every organization. Our attempts to minimize and control it are likely to help us and our organizations.

Chapter Two

Beyond Mind Reading:
The Power of Strategic Talk

Every day you make many choices about what or what not to say and how to say it. You want to be tough or soft, direct or indirect, open or secret, clear or obtuse, simple or complicated. Whether you successfully communicate in any of these ways depends not only on what you say and how you say it but also on how the other person hears it. This chapter will help you use the power of talk to make it more likely that the people you're talking to understand you the way you intend them to, regardless of the kind of message you're trying to send.

The Power of Understanding Misunderstanding

Many evenings you probably watch the next day's weather forecast on television. You know that you can't change the weather, so why do you bother? There are some very practical reasons. If you know about sunshine, rain, snow, hurricanes, tornados, hail, lightning, wind, and tides, you can make plans with more security. For instance, you might plan to go ahead with the company picnic scheduled for Saturday because there's no rain in sight, or you might book a hotel room in the city in case the airport is shut down by snow. Even though you can't change the weather, knowing the forecast gives you the power to change your own behavior. Your knowledge and understanding give you power over yourself.

Understanding misunderstanding can give you the same kind of power over yourself. You can't eliminate the indexicality and reflexivity of language, but you can change your own talk. You can overcome its vagueness and ambiguity by using the power of talk to create shared context. You can explicitly create a shared context by carefully choosing what you say and how you say it. You can use the give-and-take of conversation using specific kinds of talk to make sure that you and others understand each other.

Understanding via Talk and Shared Context

Talk and shared context make understanding each other possible. Talk makes what's going on in our heads available to others. Shared context provides the foundation for shared understanding. We create context from our knowledge, experience, understanding, imagination, desires, and practical interests and use it to interpret the meaning of what's said. We also find context in the moment of the interaction with the people, the place, the time, the purpose, and the talk itself. Context also includes what happens afterward. For example, we can always go back in light of new experience and say, "Oh, so that's what she meant."

We create the context, whether consciously or not, by picking and choosing from among alternative interpretations of the situation. We decide on the appropriate version of who, what, where, when, why, and how. More specifically, we create a context by linking the talk to factors such as the time, the occasion, the speaker and his or her biography, the place, the intentions of the speaker, and our assumptions about shared knowledge. We have to choose what's relevant and what isn't. The speaker can help us by making some of the most important contextual features explicit. But the interpretation is ultimately our own.

The most obvious part of the context is the sequence in which the words and sentences occur. When we talk, things are said one after another, in sequence. What we say hinges on what has been said before and what will be said next, by us and by others. This sequencing of talk forms an important part of the context for meaning.

In the following examples, taken from some research on doctor-patient interviews done by two sociologists, Candace West and

Richard Frankel, the patients' answers to a physician's questions seem perfectly clear:

1. *Patient:* We never had no trouble with the police.
2. *Patient:* Well, I have veins, but I don't know if they're close or not.
3. *Patient:* B-E-T-T-Y.

The grammar may not be perfect, but the answers themselves seem clear and straightforward. The first answers a question about any previous encounters with the police. The second is a discussion of the patient's veins. The third concerns the spelling or pronunciation of someone's name.

Now, as I put the answers in context by revealing the questions that preceded them, see how your understanding changes:

1. *Physician:* Have you ever had a history of cardiac arrest in your family?

   Patient: We never had no trouble with the police.
2. *Physician:* How about varicose veins?

   Patient: Well, I have veins, but I don't know if they're close or not.
3. *Physician:* What's your name?

   Patient: Betty Groff.

   Physician: How do you spell that?

   Patient: B-E-T-T-Y.

Putting the patients' replies in sequence changes their meaning for us. The physicians' questions give a new twist and a different meaning to the patients' utterances.

Public relations people often use (or misuse) sequencing to their advantage. A critic writes, "The new Broadway musical, *Ghetto Lovers*, is generally as dismal as its name, although it has some memorable melodies and two dance numbers reminiscent of

West Side Story." The billboard says, "Don't miss the new Broadway musical, Ghetto Lovers! 'MEMORABLE MELODIES' and 'DANCE NUMBERS REMINISCENT OF WEST SIDE STORY' says Jane Doe of the Daily Gazette." Taken out of context, the remarks sound quite favorable.

If you listen to people's talk, you can often hear them creating the context in the sequence of the talk itself. For example, listen to the following business meeting:

Miguel: Krystal, what's the latest on sales in Chicago?

Krystal: That new line of casual wear from Jessica is selling like hotcakes.

Jolene: I've heard it's hard to keep in stock. Let's go back and talk about the inventory control problem we seem to be having. I don't think it's the computer program that's the problem. I think it's the quality of the information we put into it.

Jolene's switch to a discussion of inventory control would sound out of place if she hadn't explicitly created a context for understanding her talk. For example, without Jolene's contextualizing utterance ("I've heard it's hard to keep in stock. Let's go back and talk about the inventory control problem we seem to be having"), the conversation would have gone like this:

Miguel: Krystal, what's the latest on sales in Chicago?

Krystal: That new line of casual wear from Jessica is selling like hotcakes.

Jolene: I don't think it's the computer program that's the problem. I think it's the quality of the information we put into it.

If Jolene hadn't put her talk in the context of inventory problems, her remarks might have made no sense to Miguel and Krystal; they wouldn't have known how to interpret them. First of all, they wouldn't have known why she jumped to talking of the computer program. Further, the company has many computers and a number of different programs used to help with payroll, employee records, accounting, taxes, orders to jobbers, sales records, fabric supply, and inventory. Without Jolene's statement, how could they know to which program or function Jolene is referring? If they're lucky, Miguel and Krystal might guess correctly; they might not. Instead, Jolene makes understanding possible by providing a context as she leads into her opening talk.

Background Knowledge Is Part of Context

We use our background knowledge, what is called taken-for-granted knowledge in ethnomethodology, to create context. The best way to demonstrate this is to take our background knowledge and breach it. A vivid and powerful example of this is seen in the story, told by Tobias Schneebaum, of a Brooklyn artist who tried to find paradise on earth living with the Akaramas, a tribe in the rain forest of Peru.

The story is a parable for the Garden of Eden story. The tropical forest provided everything the artist needed to live. It was luxuriant, warm, all enveloping, and nurturing. He felt totally at peace—except for one thing. He wanted to leave his own reality completely and become a full member of the tribe who lived in this earthly paradise. He learned their language, went naked, shaved his body hair, learned to throw a spear and use a bow and arrow; he ate, slept, and hunted with them. But he couldn't forget who he was and what he knew.

His reality was different from theirs because his knowledge was different. He knew that the whiteness on the mountains, visible from the highest point in the village, was snow and not white flowers. He couldn't take the same things for granted that they did. Their ways of living and dying were not his. They were cannibals, and he couldn't ignore his massive feelings of fear, guilt, and moral outrage about cannibalism. His own knowledge prevented a total breach of his own reality and kept the Akaramas' reality separate from his. This separation—his inability to accept and participate in cannibalism—resulted in his expulsion.

We can learn something useful about the relationship of taken-for-granted knowledge and context from this story. Our taken-for-granted knowledge provides the foundation for our experience and understanding of the world. It's part of the woodwork. We don't notice it but use it to interpret what we see and hear. To bring this knowledge from the background of our world to the foreground, we have to step out of our normal routine.

For example, imagine that you've been away from your house or apartment for a month on holiday. You've just returned and walk up to the front door, turn the key, and let yourself in. What do you notice? It smells funny! Other people's homes have a noticeable smell, but until this, you may not have noticed that yours does too. The smell is so familiar and a part of your daily life, so much a part of the foundation of your life, that it goes unnoticed until you get a chance to approach it after an absence.

We take many things for granted: names of objects, creatures, and people, including our own names; ways of doing business; ways of dressing, eating, behaving. As our world changes and we learn about others' ways, we become more sensitive to our own, taken-for-granted ways. Traveling to foreign lands makes this immediately apparent, but we don't have to look to other lands; we can find important differences close to home.

Within our own organization there are people who may have different assumptions about the organization than we do. We shouldn't assume we all share the same goals and objectives. People may have very different practical interests, or hidden agendas. Not everyone will take the same things for granted. Even if everyone is trained in the procedures, purposes, roles, rules, goals, methods, and objectives of our organization, we need to remind ourselves that not everyone will share the same taken-for-granted world.

What *does* everyone in our organization share? We can't really know in the abstract. Each time we interact, we can learn about this sharing through our communication in that moment. But any communication based on assumed sharing of goals, objectives, or knowledge that is never made explicit may fail miserably. We can't simply take shared context for granted.

When we do business with people outside our organization, what do we know about their taken-for-granted knowledge? What's the difference between what we know and what they know? How does their world fit with ours when we're talking about business? Our contexts may be so different that our interaction continually breaches each other's reality. We must make context explicit in our talk.

Understanding Requires Shared Context

We ensure shared context through talk, but not just any kind of talk. We can't use one-way communication to tell people what to do, or what we want, or what we think, and expect them to understand. They may understand, but they may not. By the time we find out, it may be too late to make ourselves clear. One-way talk doesn't give us any means for finding out if there is a shared context for understanding. For example, Figure 2.1 shows how the indexicality and reflexivity of language create barriers to knowing that the speaker's context and understanding are the same as the listener's. Unless there is opportunity for talk, back and forth, we have no way of checking. We can only wait and see what the listeners do and say subsequently and hope their understanding is what we intended.

Yet you've undoubtedly been in situations in which comments or questions were unacceptable or clearly discouraged. Consider one manager's pep talk to a department:

> The productivity in this department needs radical improvement. We've been holding everybody up because of it. I know you're all as concerned about this as I am, and I know that you can do what needs to be done to put it right. Now, I don't want any questions or comments. Just go and do what has to be done.

The manager expects people in the department to fill in the blanks. Unfortunately, the manager's one-way talk tells nothing about

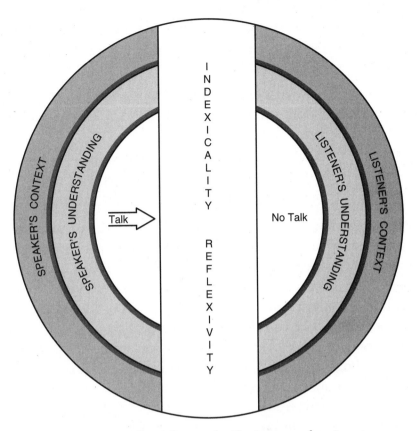

Figure 2.1. Indexicality and reflexivity are barriers to understanding in one-way talk.

what's understood. In this situation, indexicality and reflexivity remain virtually impenetrable barriers to shared understanding.

We produce shared context through talk. We give explicit information that the listener might not have, and we ask questions to make sure what we have said is understood. In the following example, Gary and Jean each have a different context for understanding what they are talking about:

Gary: Jean, I need the promotional stuff on the XLR copier for a meeting this afternoon. How soon can you get it to me?

Jean: Who are you meeting with? Which promotional stuff do you want?

Gary: What do you mean? I didn't know I had a choice.

Jean: Weren't you at the marketing meeting last week?

Gary: No. I was out of the office.

Jean: Well, we now have different material for each of the configurations we offer and for each of the different leasing packages.

Gary: Okay, give me everything so I can check it out before the meeting. And then, if you have a moment, let's talk about which ones you think would work best with this group.

When Gary first asks for promotional material, he thinks Jean will know what he's talking about. But he is wrong. Jean doesn't know exactly because she knows more than Gary does. Gary missed a meeting that gave Jean a new context for understanding by providing new information. Gary and Jean didn't understand each other because they didn't have the same information about the promotional material. Once this difference was apparent, the misunderstanding was solvable through questions and answers.

This misunderstanding happened for three reasons. First, Jean and Gary couldn't read each other's mind. Second, the words they were using had many possible meanings and had to be interpreted. And third, they each had a different context for understanding. Jean's questions about the meaning of Gary's request exposed their different contexts and opened the way to understanding.

Although most of us don't consciously realize that all clear communication depends on shared context, our talk shows that we do recognize it on some level. Whenever we say to someone, "Well, it all depends . . . ," we show that we know that meaning depends on context. When I talk to my co-workers about a project that we have been working on together for three weeks, I talk about it in a way that draws on this involvement. I can hold them accountable for already knowing certain details. I don't have to spell everything out.

It's the same as two old friends meeting over lunch in a restaurant. They can talk in "shorthand" because they share certain background knowledge. Someone overhearing their conversation might hear the following exchange:

Phoebe: Did you hear about Victor and Emily?

Jane: Yes, and I think it's wonderful.

Phoebe: But quite a surprise.

Jane: So was mine.

Phoebe: But you were older.

Phoebe and Jane know that they're talking about an unexpected pregnancy. But what do we outsiders know? We have to fill in what's missing to make the talk understandable. We can't really understand the talk without knowing all the experiences that Phoebe and Jane share. They can chat like this for hours, and we would still be in the dark.

But even when we don't share a context as Phoebe and Jane do, we're still quite good at finding some shared context with almost anyone. At the bus stop we can talk about the weather with a perfect stranger. At a cocktail party we can talk with people about sports, movies, restaurants, or vacations. But the more complicated the communication, the more it depends on extensive shared context. And when clear communication is important, we shouldn't just assume that we share a context. We better make sure that we do.

Creating Shared Context with Talk

We find out how much we share with others by knowing as much about their individual backgrounds as we can and by talking and listening to them and watching what they do. When we start conversations, we guess at what the other people already know. If we didn't, we wouldn't know how to begin or what to say. If we assume the other person knows more than he really does, we'll be talking over his head; if we assume she knows less than she really does, we'll be talking down to her.

One way to hear how talk creates shared context is by showing how children's talk differs from adults' talk. Being a grown-up means sounding like a grown-up. And that means being skilled at guessing, or finding out, how much the person you're talking to already knows. Adult-child conversations often sound like this one between Vicky (an adult) and Johnny (a five-year-old child):

Vicky: Hello. What's your name?

Johnny: Johnny. You know what?

Vicky: What?

Johnny: Mary took my crayon and won't give it back, and I
    got Marion to tell her mom but she had to go to the grocery.

Johnny sounds like a child because his talk doesn't seem sensitive to what Vicky knows, or needs to know, to understand his story. He talks as though Vicky already had enough background knowledge to understand even though it was their first meeting. He assumes that Vicky knows who Mary is; who Marion is; what the relationship of Mary, Marion, and Johnny is; how the incident began; what Marion was supposed to tell her mom and why; and so on. Since Vicky just met Johnny, there is little chance that she knows any of this. She can't make any good sense of Johnny's talk until she starts asking questions to fill in all the information she doesn't know.

Most adults don't sound like children, because they understand more about shared context. Young children seem to assume that everyone knows as much as they do about their world: they always use the et cetera principle. As children grow up they start to sound like adults as they get better at guessing what the people they are talking to already know.

But as adults, we also make mistakes about context when we misuse or overuse the et cetera principle and assume a shared context that either doesn't exist or isn't used. The problem is that something has to go wrong before we realize that we don't share a context. We can prevent this by talking, because the talk itself can create the context for its own understanding.

Speakers Must Listen and Listeners Must Speak

Listening skills are obviously important. Many organizations worry about misunderstanding when working with clients and look to effective listening as a critical technique. Poor listening can happen because people block out what they don't want to hear, they are distracted, they talk rather than listen, and they're not aware of good communications skills. We can practice listening. We can even tape our phone calls to see who does most of the talking and how much of the message we understood the first time.

But better listening doesn't do away with the need to interpret meaning. You can control your own listening, but what can you do about others'? You can't control or even know about others' listening without talking to them or observing the outcome of your talk with them. If people just listen but never have the chance to talk, we can know how they understood us only from what they do. And they might do it wrong because they didn't understand, or they might do it right, but for the wrong reason.

Good listening is necessary for understanding, but it doesn't guarantee it. We can't understand what we don't hear. But we make our hearing public when we talk, not when we listen. To emphasize one at the expense of the other would be a mistake. We have to take turns listening and talking, as listener and speaker, to make our understanding explicit.

However, not all talking creates shared context. Figure 2.2 presents a diagram of a conversation in which talk doesn't necessarily create a shared context for meaning because the speakers don't consciously use their talk to remedy the problems indexicality and reflexivity create. They don't reduce the ambiguity of their talk by using specific kinds of talk to work through the meaning of what's said. Although talk in which the participants take turns talking and listening is definitely an improvement over the techniques illustrated in Figure 2.1, in itself it's not enough. It's what most of our talk is like before we understand misunderstanding. Simply talking back and forth doesn't necessarily tell us what each of us understands. We

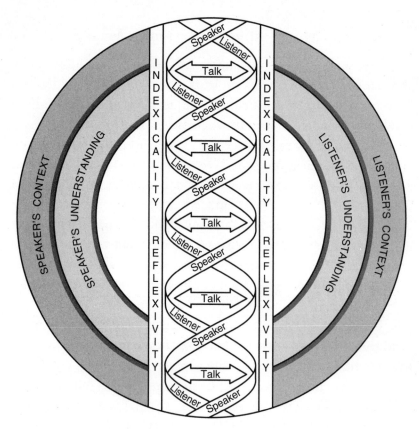

Figure 2.2. Indexicality and reflexivity are barriers to
understanding when context isn't explicit.

have to consciously use special strategies in our turn as speaker to
make what we understood as listener, or what we want the listener
to understand, explicit in our talk. Unless we do so, we can't be sure
of shared context or understanding.

Strategic Talk as a Path to Shared Understanding

We can cope with the indexical and reflexive nature of language
by taking turns as speaker and listener as the talk unfolds over time.
By doing this and by using particular kinds of talk—namely formulations, questions and answers, paraphrasing, examples, and stories—we can achieve shared understanding by making shared

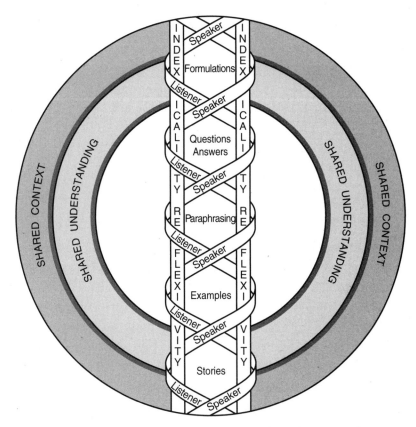

Figure 2.3. Strategic talk creates a shared context for understanding.

context explicit. I call this *strategic talk* as a way of emphasizing that consciously using these techniques with a full understanding of why misunderstanding happens will help you remedy vagueness and ambiguity caused by the indexicality and reflexivity of language. Figure 2.3 presents a graphic view of how strategic talk works at clarifying meaning by making context and interpretation explicit.

The elements of strategic talk are familiar to all of us. They are not new discoveries of ethnomethodology or conversation analysis. But using them in the full knowledge of the indexical and reflexive nature of language makes them special. Such an approach involves us in the social construction of context and meaning as we take turns as speaker and listener working at making sense of each other. Using these kinds of talk is part of the work we have to do to make sense of our organizational lives. It shows that we recognize that the burden of responsibility falls on each of us to work at creating the context for understanding the organizational world in which we live. Although all language is interpretation and we have no absolute remedy for language's vagueness and equivocality, we can, for all practical purposes, create a shared context for understanding by systematically using strategic talk.

Formulations

In the jargon of ethnomethodology, as explained by Harold Garfinkel and Harvey Sacks, we call the first kind of strategic talk *formulations*. Formulations label, or sum up, the talk. They reflexively create the context of the talk by saying, in so many words, what we or others are talking about, when we are talking, why we are talking, who is talking, who we are, where we are, what we are doing, and how.

When formulations describe, explain, characterize, explicate, translate, summarize, or give the gist of what was said, they tell us how we're to understand the context we're in as well as the meaning of what's being said in that situation. When we formulate talk we actually step outside the conversation and tell people what they should understand us to be saying in the conversation. We're telling people our interpretation and it gives them the chance to say (to themselves, or out loud), "Ahh, so that's what you're talking about." They can then say, "That's what I thought" or "That's not what I heard you saying." Formulations are incredibly useful ways of checking understanding. People use formulations in ordinary conversation, meetings, training sessions, radio and television interviews and talk shows—in short, every situation in which people talk to one another. Formulations take the general form of "So what you're saying is . . ." or "Now I want to talk about. . . ."

Earlier in the chapter, we saw Jolene use this technique as she set up a conversation about inventory control problems. Here is another example of how formulations are used. Mary is a senior manager of a large manufacturing company. John is one of her junior managers. One morning John walks into Mary's office and begins telling her about a problem that has come to a head that morning in the shipping department:

> *John: I want to talk about a problem with you.*
>
> *Mary:* What is it?
>
> *John:* It looks like the union might shut down the shipping department tomorrow because of that action we took on absenteeism last week.
>
> *Mary:* How serious is it?
>
> *John:* Unless we get someone down there to smooth the situation over, they'll walk.
>
> *Mary: So you're saying you want me to talk to Bill, the main union guy down there.*
>
> *John:* I think that would be best.
>
> *Mary: Are you telling me that you can't handle it?*
>
> *John:* I could try, but with your experience I think you would have a better chance of straightening this all out.

There are three formulations in this brief conversation; each one is italicized. First, John tells Mary that she should hear the talk that follows as talk about a problem. Second, Mary gives John her interpretation of his reporting the problem to her as his way of saying she should talk to the union steward. And third, Mary tells John that she hears him saying he cannot solve the problem himself. All of these formulations are done by the participants saying out loud their interpretations of the meaning of the talk that is going on. Obviously much of the background has been left unsaid. Therefore, instead of leaving the understanding of the talk up to chance, the speakers give their interpretations explicitly.

The fact that we all use formulations in our everyday talk shows that we already know that we cannot leave understanding to chance. If we want to be sure people hear what we are saying in a certain way, then we formulate it by saying something like, "I want to tell you about. . . ." If we want to check our interpretation of what we heard, we formulate it by saying, "So what you're saying is. . . ." But even though we already use formulations, our communication will be helped by becoming more consciously aware of them. Once we know how formulations work, we can use them whenever we have to be absolutely sure that we understand each other. We will understand that unless we use formulations, we risk misunderstanding.

Here's another example. The interviewer on a current events TV program has just asked the distinguished guest what she thinks of the current state of Middle East peace talks. The guest replies at some length, and the interviewer says, "So what you're saying is that you think they're doomed to failure unless the Israelis are willing to give up some land." The guest replies, "No, that's not what I was saying. I said that I think. . . ."

The interviewer said how he interpreted the guest's remarks; the guest explained that his interpretation was inaccurate. If the interviewer hadn't given his interpretation out loud, then he and the guest would have assumed he understood when, in fact, he didn't. This might have important consequences later in the program. And if the interviewer misunderstood, the viewers may also have misunderstood. The formulation and the guest's response give everyone a chance to check on their interpretation.

Formulations provide an opportunity for others to say yes or no to our interpretation and to give us theirs. From that point on, people can talk further to help clarify the meaning. Formulations are an invaluable tool for ensuring clear communication. We can now make them part of our conscious repertoire of talk and use them whenever needed.

Questions and Answers

Questions and answers are an important part of strategic talk. They go as far as language can go in telling us what people understand. What is clear and obvious to us may not always be clear and obvious to others. We can assess people's answers to our questions to determine their understanding; often it takes a series of questions and answers to clear up misunderstandings.

In business, asking questions can be one of our most difficult tasks because people think language is basically clear and unambiguous and expect us to understand them the first time. We also have it ingrained in us that asking questions exposes some deficiency in the speaker or the listener. Therefore, if we ask questions, it's because we weren't listening or don't know what we should know. Even worse, we're implying that the speaker wasn't clear. In any case, most people act as though needing to ask questions is someone's fault. Once we understand that talk is indexical and reflexive, we know why questions are necessary. In most situations, unless we ask questions we don't have a hope of being sure we understand. Any situation in which we are discouraged from asking questions invites misunderstanding. Think, for example, of the manager whose pep talk said there were to be no questions or comments; what were those employees to do?

We've all been in situations where we were afraid to ask questions about things we really didn't understand because we thought our lack of understanding was our own fault. In college you may have had a professor or two who would drone on and on about ideas or theories that had not been clearly explained in the text and which were not made any more clear in class.

You had plenty of questions, but how many times did you or anybody else ask them in class? Almost never? Why? Probably because you thought asking a question would make you look foolish. And since nobody else was asking a question, you assumed that everyone else understood. Asking a question in front of everybody would have threatened your self-esteem. It was only later that you found out that nobody else understood.

Because questions demand answers, they are the best tool we have for checking our own and other's understanding. People feel compelled to answer questions they are asked. Imagine a situation in which your associate asks you the following question: "Why do you think this is the best way to market this machine?" Could you just stand there and not answer? If you did, your associate would be justified in drawing certain conclusions. Perhaps you didn't hear the question, or you heard it but were afraid to answer because you hadn't thought it through, or you were ignoring your associate, or you didn't know the answer. Questions demand an answer. If we don't hear that answer, we begin to make up reasons for its absence.

Here's another exchange to illustrate the power of questions. Adam is a senior manager for new product development, and Carol is director of marketing.

> *Carol:* That's the plan for our meeting with the advertising group.
>
> *Adam:* I think it should work very well.
>
> *Carol:* How do you see it fitting your plans?

Carol's question puts the responsibility on Adam to show that he understands. He now has the responsibility for putting Carol's plan in his own context. If she didn't take the trouble to ask the question, she couldn't be sure that he understood. Any time understanding a plan is crucial and there is no room for error, people have to ask questions to hear how everybody else understands.

Paraphrasing

Like formulations and questions and answers, paraphrasing gives others the opportunity to hear how you made sense of what they were saying. Putting other's talk into our own words, *paraphrasing*, makes our understanding of other's talk explicit. We all use paraphrasing sometimes, but in strategic talk we do it as a matter of regular practice.

Paraphrasing is especially well suited to the restaurant business. Restaurants depend on good food, good drinks, good service, good prices, and goodwill. Getting reservations and food and drink orders correct is critical to that goodwill. To help assure accuracy, staff are often trained to paraphrase the reservations and orders. This practice serves three purposes. First, it's a hearable check of the person's understanding. Second, it gives the customer the chance to affirm, change, or correct the reservation or order. And third, it makes everyone accountable for understanding because everyone heard what was said and repeated. Sharing their wishes and interpretations through paraphrasing allows customers and staff to compare their understandings instead of simply hoping that the others understood. As a result of their interchange, staff and customers can have confidence that the reservations and meals will be as planned.

Examples

Language is generally imprecise because it's indexical and reflexive. While that allows us to make sense of a wide range of information, it means that everything we say is, to some extent, a generalization. Whatever we talk about, whatever we describe, we can always say more to narrow down and be more precise about what we're saying. The best way to move from the general to the particular is to give specific examples of what we're talking about.

Why is it that "a picture is worth a thousand words"? The picture is not talk about something—it is the thing the talk is about. Talk about the picture is still talk, and we could spend the rest of our lives without explaining it perfectly or describing every detail that exists. But seeing the picture lets us make sense of the talk; it creates a context for interpreting the talk.

Strategic talk uses examples to create a context for interpretation. When pictures or objects are not available or are inappropriate, examples in words are the next best thing. Suppose I ask you to tell me about your organization. Where would you begin and where would you end? The number of things you could tell me about it is inexhaustible. You would probably ask, "What do you want to know?" Once you narrow down what my interests are, you can start giving me concrete examples from your organization. This ties your description to specific instances and gives your description a context that I can relate to from my own experience.

If you say that your company is a great place to work, I might be surprised by your enthusiasm and want to know more. I could start by asking for examples of what makes it so great. If I remain skeptical and think there must be a downside, I might ask for an example of something you'd like to change about the company. The examples you choose will tell me a bit about you and about the company.

In another context, in a different telling, the same example might become part of a story. This puts the instance being described in a very explicit context that the listener can use as a resource for interpretation.

Stories

When you tell someone a story to illustrate the meaning of what you're talking about, you make your ideas concrete and alive by embedding them in people, places, things, and time. It's no accident that we have the expression "Let me tell you a story to show you what I mean" in our language. Perhaps you already use stories to improve understanding. But now, with the conscious knowledge of why they are critical, you'll be more inclined to use stories consistently.

In telling a story, you show your understanding of a person, event, idea, program, problem, or solution, for example. In listening to others' stories, you decide whether their understanding fits yours. We can tell a story to show that we understood someone else's story. To do this we try to make our story parallel to the first story in all its essential parts. For example, suppose you tell a story about what happened in a recent meeting. In telling the story, you provide the details of a disagreement between one of the executives and the manager of another division of the company: "Listen to what happened in the meeting this morning. Mary and Bob really got at one another. She thought Bob's new marketing approach was all wrong. And she told him so. He didn't like it one bit. But I think she's right on."

Then someone in the group you're talking with pipes in, saying, "You know, the same thing happened to me last week." That person continues, saying, "I had a meeting with Ethel and Maria. What a waste of time it was with those two arguing back and forth about production schedules."

The second story does not reflect the point you meant to make with yours. You are therefore faced with choices. You could drop the subject and completely avoid embarrassing the story teller. Or you could express interest in the story, and then cycle back to yours, saying, "I understand your frustration in wasted time, but the difference is that what I saw Bob and Mary doing seemed very constructive." In any event, your story presents your talk in a specific context that helps listeners narrow down its possible meanings. They can show their interpretation in their second story. We can then work with this to straighten out any hearable misunderstandings.

Informed Action

One of the most important goals of strategic talk is informed action. Informed action means doing a job as we're supposed to, with shared understanding of the full meaning of what counts as doing it right. It means achieving the highest possible level of operational efficiency and reliability. It means optimizing human, physical, and capital resources in doing the organization's work. This is a goal every organization wants to reach. Using the power of strategic talk can help us achieve it. Certain instances may require only some aspects of strategic talk; others, particularly when understanding is critical or the issues complicated, may demand that each technique be enlisted.

Summary

A solution to the problem of misunderstanding caused by the indexicality and reflexivity of language lies in using the power of strategic talk to create a shared context for understanding. This way of understanding communication can make an extraordinary difference to your personal and professional life. When your understanding of misunderstanding changes, your world changes along with it. You can no longer take understanding for granted. Communication problems that were previously a source of frustration, embarrassment, and inconvenience now have an explanation and a solution.

In order to understand each other, we need to create a shared context through talk. Shared context means having the same basis for interpreting people's talk that they intended us to have. All possible elements of context, those that we bring to the situation as well as those we find there, exist for all practical purposes in the moment of the situation. When we talk to others, we have to assume they already have a knowledge base that allows us to talk in the first place. For example, we assume that they know we are talking to them and, if we are talking in English, that they understand English. We might also assume that they know something about who we are, what we are talking about, where we are, when we are talking to them, why we are talking to them, and so on. All of these aspects can be called the context of our talk.

Misunderstanding talk most often happens when we assume that both parties share the who, what, where, when, why, and how of the situation. If we both work in the same organization, we're likely to assume that the other knows as much as we do about everything that goes on that relates to doing the job. Working for the same organization obviously helps people share a context about some things—but not about everything. Without the same context, we can't be completely sure that we share understanding. In fact, we can't be sure we share a context for understanding with anyone—whether boss, colleague, friend, lover, or spouse—until we see that what we have discussed turns out right or wrong.

As speaker and listener we can use strategic talk to prevent misunderstanding by assuring that we have the right context. Strategic talk is necessary for several reasons. First, no matter how much we think we know about the people we're talking to, they may be relying on ideas or facts that we don't know as a context for understanding. Second, we can know people's context only from what they say and do. Third, people's words and actions may be based on reasons that are very different from what we suppose they are. Even their talk and actions don't automatically tell us about shared context. But as long as things work out, this is not a problem. Finally, in normal, everyday life, best guesses about shared context may be good enough. But in critical situations, they aren't.

With these ideas in mind, we see that strategic talk is crucial if we are to improve our chances of understanding. We must use formulations, questions and answers, paraphrasing, examples, and stories systematically to create shared context and shared understanding and make it explicit. These are normal kinds of talk that we already use in our everyday lives; now that we know their power, we must also use them consciously.

Checklist Part One

Recognize that misunderstanding is normal because talk is routinely vague and ambiguous.

Know that you can't eliminate the features of language that may make it unclear and easily misunderstood: indexicality (the meaning of language depends on the context) and reflexivity (the fact that we are responsible for creating the context). Understanding misunderstanding gives you power over your own talk.

Understand that people trust you to fill in the correct meaning for what they say even when they are not precise.

Understand that people don't realize they are not precise.

Recognize that context—which includes background knowledge, experience, understanding, imagination, desires, practical interests, the moment of the interaction, the people, the place, gestures, body positions, intonation, the time, the purpose, the talk itself, and what happens afterward—gives meaning to everything we say or write.

Appreciate the extent to which avoiding misunderstanding can improve the bottom line, and take steps to that end.

Solve the problem of misunderstanding by creating a shared context for understanding through talk.

Take turns as speaker and listener to make your understanding explicit.

Know that it is your responsibility to use strategic talk—formulations, questions and answers, paraphrasing, examples, and stories—to create shared context.

Part Two

---

*How You Can
Increase the Odds
in Your Favor*

Chapter Three

When Words Are Deeds: Talk That Makes Work Happen

This chapter should help you use talk to make work happen the way you want it to happen. It can give you the knowledge and techniques, but you still have to decide when and where to apply them: your talk must be appropriate to the context in which you find yourself. You always have the responsibility to decide what every new situation is and what kind of talk it calls for.

The examples in this book are of people trying to understand and be understood. They provide a sampling of situations in which strategic talk can be used in an appropriate and sensitive way. Using strategic talk isn't always easy. We have to train ourselves to do it. As we've seen, people expect us to fill in meaning for them and can get quite annoyed when we ask them to be more precise. So using strategic talk can make us feel funny at first. Some typical feelings include these:

Fear: "If I ask too many questions I'm sure I'll be fired."

Anger: "Why don't they realize that what they're saying needs some concrete examples if they really want me to understand what they mean?"

Guilt: "I know they think they're being perfectly clear, but I don't get it. Maybe I need to work harder."

Embarrassment: "I hope they don't think I'm stupid."

Inadequacy: "Maybe I'm in the wrong job. Everyone else seems to understand."

Powerlessness: "No matter how hard I try, I still feel I'm missing something. I just don't know what to do."

Relief: "At least my boss is beginning to realize I can't read her mind. It sure makes my job a lot easier."

Pride: "Now that people in the office understand misunderstanding, efficiency and morale have really improved."

Until the people you're talking to understand misunderstanding and are aware of language's indexicality and reflexivity, they may wonder why you don't understand. We have to use strategic talk in spite of—and to compensate for—this gap in their understanding.

Using Talk for Action

Many people say they want to develop better strategies for communicating with colleagues; they might say, "I've got to learn to clarify what we talk about so there aren't so many misunderstandings." But how? We give people directions, orders, promises, requests, commitments, objections, excuses, agreements, policies, or goals when we want to get jobs done. Are these ways of talking possible solutions to the problem? They're *part of* the solution. But they *become* the solution only when we see that they're also part of the problem, once we recognize their indexicality and know how to remedy it.

Talk and Policies

Suppose we give our employees a simple company policy: "Every order must be filled and sent out within twenty-four hours of receipt." How should our employees understand this policy? What does it mean in practice?

- Does it tell employees how to do their daily jobs so that the policy is carried out?

- Does it mean that employees must send out every order within twenty-four hours even if it's incomplete?

- Does it mean that it's the employees' responsibility to see that this policy is followed?
- Does it mean employees should do whatever is needed to make the rule work even if it's not within their job description?
- Does it mean changing or modifying employees' jobs so the policy can work?

We might simply say that the employees should just use their own common sense to take care of the order, but our idea of common sense may not be theirs. Policies rely on language, and, like all language, we can't make sense of policies without interpretation. And different people may interpret them differently. Therefore, we won't risk this step.

Informed action can come from creating a shared context using the formulations, questions and answers, paraphrasings, examples, and stories of strategic talk. If we want people to understand a twenty-four-hour turnaround policy, then we and our employees should jointly create the context in which this translates into action. Do this by talking it through. Give employees the opportunity to ask questions: "What if this happens? What do I do then?" Or "How do I prioritize orders if it's clear that we don't have enough employees to do the job because someone's out sick?" Answer employees' questions by giving examples: "Here's an example of what we're expecting. . . ." People understand policies by hearing what's said and then filling in all the details and background information that were left unsaid. Confusion arises when people don't realize that policies are not self-explanatory, because they don't tell us all that we need to know to carry them out.

Talk and Tasks

Job assignments work the same way as new policies. When you're given new work to do, how clearly do you understand what's to be done? You want to be able to clarify the instructions to avoid misunderstanding. But what if you're expected to understand, to fill in the blanks, without always saying, "What exactly do you want?"

This expectation can get in the way of understanding if it makes you afraid to clarify points you don't understand.

Imagine that you received the following message from your boss on your voice mail: "Go through all the files and reports you can find on our competition's sales in the regions we want to move into and let me know by next Tuesday what you think our approach should be." If some significant questions come to mind, you can use strategic talk. First, formulate the talk by saying something like, "This may seem an odd request since I've worked for this company for six years, but I want to be sure I understand exactly what you want so I don't waste your time or mine. So let me ask you a few simple questions."

Then, ask questions: "Can I discuss this project with anyone else before I come back to you with it?" "Does this list I've drafted include all of the regions in which you're interested?" "Do you want to get any reports on my progress as I go along?"

Paraphrase: "So let me make sure I'm hearing you right. You want me to. . . ."

Ask for examples: "Do you want this to be like the report I did last year?" "What do you want this to look like when I'm done?"

Tell stories: "I remember researching the East Coast market for you. You really liked the approach I used. We got some people from finance and marketing involved right at the start to prevent problems later on. Any objections to my doing that again?"

You may be thinking that if you responded in this way—or even if you used only a few of the strategic talk techniques—your boss would think you were slow and probably let you go. That's precisely the problem. We're afraid to use strategic talk for fear of the consequences. But if you're unclear on how to proceed in a project, then you have to use at least some of these techniques—or take your chances on wasting everyone's time and money. The strategies you use are up to you. But you better use some.

Talk and Rules

Like policies and assignments, rules are an important part of every organization. We need them. Rules make us all accountable for certain kinds of behavior. We have rules for appraising performance, making office assignments, ordering equipment, dealing with clients, taking coffee breaks, preparing expense reports, and scheduling vacations. Most of us think that rules tell us what to do and that once we know the rules, we will know how to act. However, the way we actually use rules is not quite that simple.

Sociologist John Heritage gives us an interesting and useful picture of how rules work in our everyday lives. He uses the example of a rule that all adults in our society should know and understand, to show us how rules, like all language, are indexical and reflexive. The rule, which he calls the "Greetings Rule," is "When greeted, return the greeting." Heritage hasn't invented this rule. We all know it and use it. If I asked you what you were supposed to do if someone said hello to you, you would probably say, "I'd say 'hello' back." It's part of our socialization.

But suppose you have to work late one night and don't leave the office until 1:30 in the morning. As you're going to your car, a man you've never seen before steps out of the shadows and says, "Hi." What do you do? Do you say hello back to him? Or do you ignore him, quickly get into your car, lock the doors and drive away? How do you make sense of the norm in this situation? The rule has changed from "When greeted, return the greeting" to "When greeted, return the greeting, unless you are greeted late at night by someone you don't know." Suppose the person who steps out of the shadows is your CEO. What is the norm? It has changed again. Now it reads, "When greeted, return the greeting, unless you are greeted late at night by someone you don't know, unless that person is your CEO, in which case return the greeting."

Consider another example. You are walking down the corridor of your office building and you run into a manager you had a strong disagreement with earlier that day. He says "Hello." What do you do? Your decision whether to return the greeting will define the present relationship between you and the manager. It will convey how you currently feel about the argument and how you want the manager to understand your feelings. If you say "Hi," it may mean that you are ready to restore your relationship to normal or at least ready to talk some more. By returning the greeting you have given the manager the chance to say something back to you. You have created a situation in which further talk is possible.

You create the opposite situation when you ignore the greeting and just carry on walking down the corridor. If the manager knows you have heard and seen him, your message says, "I don't have anything to say to you." And that is literally true. The manager may try to get you to talk, but you can continue to ignore him. In that case the relationship hasn't been restored, and there is no opportunity for further talk at this point.

So, what is the rule now? Maybe it goes something like this:

The rule is "When greeted, return the greeting." But there are many times when we don't follow the rule. In fact we never follow it automatically. We can't, because the rule, itself, doesn't tell us when to use it. We have to decide in each moment of our lives when to return a greeting with a greeting. Nobody can give us enough rules to tell us what to do each time. Every greeting has to be understood on its own terms. Our understanding of it will tell us what to do, even if our conclusion is that we don't know what to do in that situation.

This doesn't mean that there is no rule for greetings. It means that even though we know the rule, we still have the job of making sense of it in each new situation using what we bring to the situation and what we find there. The kind of greeting we give reflexively creates the situation just as the situation creates the greeting we give. The rule doesn't automatically tell us what to do, just as a twenty-four-hour turnaround policy doesn't tell a company's employees how to achieve the policy in every minute of their working days. The rule needs to be considered in each instance and interpreted in the context of the situation. The rule, after all, is expressed in language.

Employers who expect that providing employees with a set of rules will enable everyone in the organization to understand things in the same way and to behave in a prescribed manner will be sorely disappointed. We make sense of rules by interpreting their meaning in context. To ensure the same interpretation, we have to ensure the same context. This means using strategic talk to create shared context for understanding. In the imperfect world of communication through language, we have to expect a certain amount of misunderstanding. Policies, assignments, and rules are always necessarily incomplete because more can always be said. In important situations more *must* be said. And it must be said each time. Even when talk is clarified for a particular occasion, on the next occasion it must often be clarified again.

Talking Within the Organization

An officer of a large corporation was concerned about misunderstanding between management and employees over the use of the organization's performance appraisal system. "I undertook a purge of what I call 'middle-management gobbledygook,' language used by managers that doesn't communicate to employees a clear evaluation of their performance." According to the officer, these managers muddle clear directions on how employees should improve their work. When they do that, they stifle initiative, creativity, and innovation in those people on their way up from the lower echelons of the bank. He continued, saying "I told these managers that they better learn to say what they mean. Employees need to clearly understand the quality of their job performance. One of the managers, who was a kind of spokesperson for all of them, claimed that they were very clear in what they said. But the feedback I get shows that the employees misunderstand them. I told her that they all better learn to speak so they could be clearly understood. But, to be honest, I'm not sure I could tell them how to do that."

Aspects of strategic talk can help here. Performance appraisal systems make much more sense when they give examples of the kind of performance they try to measure. Supervisors and employees can talk about performance examples right from the start. They need to discuss each other's understanding of what counts as the job. Concrete examples from management of specific items in the job description and in the performance appraisal system make the job come alive. Examples from employees tell supervisors how well employees understand the job. These examples should be supplemented with questions and answers from both parties. Supervisors can tell stories about how other employees have done the job and about how an ideal employee would. Such talk enhances understanding and can help make misunderstanding explicit.

Clarity about job performance and expectations is critical to people's health. A young woman came close to having a nervous breakdown because of a misunderstanding about her job. She was such an excellent manager that her boss kept piling on new responsibilities. She thought she had once understood the range and limits of the job, but now she had no idea. When she told her boss that she no longer knew where her job began and ended, her boss said, "You've just misunderstood the situation. All of this is part of the job. You have to be flexible." She was given more and more responsibility until she finally cried out in anguish, "What do they want from me?" This is a cry of frustration, but it is also a cry of misunderstanding.

Understanding our responsibilities can be a problem in all organizations at all levels. Expect misunderstanding and you will also know what to do about it. Formulate your expectations quite explicitly. You might say, "These are the tasks that I see you doing and these are the tasks that I will do." Ask questions: "Does that make sense to you?" Give examples: "Here are some examples of what has to be done." Tell stories: "Let me tell you about the last time we did this kind of job for someone." Keep at it with strategic talk.

Obligations and responsibilities change as relationships and conditions change over time. Talk must be ongoing, and channels of communication must be open between people. At crucial times we must sit down and talk face-to-face about what has happened and what is supposed to happen. Misunderstandings can be clarified and time and money saved. It takes time, but it's worth it.

Talking Outside the Organization

Every organization uses policies, rules, and regulations to keep business running smoothly. Employees in the organization see them as routine and make sense of them, even though different employees may interpret them in very different ways. As insiders, they know these policies, rules, and regulations, their purpose, and how to work them. Outsiders can often experience these same policies, rules, and regulations as arbitrary and as impenetrable barricades. Why? Because outsiders' context for understanding is different.

When we do business with people outside our organization, we can accomplish tasks more efficiently if we can get people to share our context for understanding. We can use strategic talk to eliminate significant misunderstandings with people who are outside the organization. We can talk with them until we hear that they understand the things that are critical to them.

The mayor of a municipal council, negotiating a $200 million international investment deal, found that the deal was about to come off the rails. People seemed to misunderstand exactly what was on the table for negotiation and what was nonnegotiable. The mayor found out the hard way that there's a need to clarify the expectations of all parties to avoid unnecessary complications. When the council realized that the investing company misunderstood the conditions for rezoning the land where its factory was to be built, it put the deal on hold. This cost the city and the company a lot of time and money. If they're successful at getting everyone back to the table, the mayor will have to work to make sure that everyone understands each other. The mayor knows that misunderstanding in situations like this is too expensive.

Anticipating misunderstanding between insiders and outsiders can go a long way toward solving it. Don't assume that the parties to a negotiation understand what you understand until they show that they do explicitly in their talk. If you don't hear their understanding out loud, don't assume that it exists. Be sure to use lots of concrete examples to illustrate the terms and implications of the agreement. Above all, expect misunderstanding at any stage of the negotiations. And throughout the negotiations, continue to liberally use the conversational devices of strategic talk to make everyone's understanding explicit.

The president of an advertising agency found that not clearly dividing responsibilities between itself and its clients often led to misunderstanding and a waste of time and money. "Clients often don't understand what we will do for them and what they have to do for themselves," he observed. "In a recent job we did for a local car dealership, we assumed that the clients understood that it was their job to determine the key concepts that we were to communicate to the consumer. But they assumed that we would do it. We only discovered this misunderstanding after a number of days had been wasted, and their whole campaign lost valuable momentum. It made me realize that we have to work harder at clearly communicating the division of work to our clients to avoid that kind of misunderstanding."

Understanding the Customer's Needs and Desires

Professional salespeople have extensive experience with misunderstanding. They must be able to recognize when a customer misunderstands what they are saying and how to clear it up. Salespeople know that misunderstanding happens all the time, in part because they can't always be sure of the customer's frame of reference or context. Although some salespeople claim to be good at reading the customer's mind, most can't and don't rely on that skill. Instead, they work with what the customer says. They're not surprised at how often they think the customer is saying one thing and find out later that the customer meant something else.

Good salespeople know that selling means talking and showing. It takes time. They have to understand the customer's needs and desires, as well as constraints, in order to get people to buy what they want to sell. If we listen to sales conversations, we can hear people using many of the conversational devices covered earlier.

"How can I help you?"	A greeting opens up the possibility of further talk.
"I'm looking for a new car."	This rules out buying a used car.
"What did you have in mind?"	Narrows down the context.
"I really like the Cavalier."	Context is made narrower but still open-ended.
"We have quite a few on the lot with different option packages and different colors. Why don't we go outside and look at some? When we find one you like, you can take it out for a drive."	Lots of examples to see and choose from to narrow down the selection.
"I know pretty much what I'm looking for. A Z24 with automatic and air."	Now we're getting down to specifics, but there is still some open-enedness regarding interior and other options.
"I have three Z24s that I can show you. I just sold a black Z24 this morning to a nice young business-woman like yourself. She traded in her sedan for this great sporty little car. Will you be looking to do a trade-in?"	More narrowing down with a story to suggest additional context in the form of the prospective buyer's identity. Creating a context for making a deal.
"I do have a trade-in. But I'm considering a lease deal through my company."	The business context is correct and the trade-in will be a consideration.

The conversation creates the context for understanding the customer. Salespeople may be talking to people they know and have dealt with before or to strangers. In either case, they have to create a context for the sale. Their talk reflexively finds and creates that context. Customer understanding of the product or service and salesperson understanding of need or desire can't be taken for granted. Formulations, questions and answers, paraphrasing, examples, and stories can all ensure that understanding.

Asking Questions of the Marketplace

Our world seems to place a high value on scientific knowledge and little value on common sense knowledge. We try to use scientific methods for managing all aspects of our organizations, including production, marketing, sales, and our way of communicating. The logic of scientific investigation demands that what we want to know about is clearly defined, that we can know exactly what it is and what it isn't. Yet many of the areas of interest to organizations can't be clearly defined in this way because they aren't physical objects. Instead, they are such variables as customer preference and desire rather than customer height and blood pressure.

Consider a favorite organizational research tool, the market survey. These surveys use "scientific instruments," such as questionnaires, to measure people's preferences, likes, dislikes, attitudes, motives, prejudices, and so on. They do this by administering questions that have been pre- and posttested for validity (they must measure what they claim to be measuring) and reliability (they must measure it accurately and consistently).

Rather than present a long, detailed explanation of why these instruments aren't truly scientific, and why they can't be valid or reliable in more than a common sense way, here's an example of what happens when one actually administers a survey and tries to understand the results.

A poll has been developed to gather views on the economic and political state of the nation. In this poll, people selected at random are asked a series of questions over the phone. The answers are added together and said to represent national opinion on a variety of political and economic issues. Those who designed the poll claim that this small sample of interviews fairly represents the entire population. Questions include these:

1. I would now like to ask about the pace of change in the country. Do you feel things are changing
   ____ Too quickly
   ____ Too slowly
   ____ Just about the right pace
   ____ Don't know

2. Over the past year, has the economic situation for you and your family
   ____ Gotten much better
   ____ Gotten slightly better
   ____ Stayed about the same
   ____ Gotten slightly worse
   ____ Gotten much worse
   ____ Not sure/don't know

In my seminars on organizational communication, I ask people to answer the questions in the poll and to write down how they understood the questions. In a room of twenty people, I often hear twenty different meanings for the same question; but since only a few choices are given as answers, many of the answers are the same. Here some examples of the different meanings people have given to question 1:

- The question is asking about environmental policy.
- The question is asking about the economy, social system, and world image.
- The question is asking about technology.
- The question is asking about government institutions.

- The question is asking about the economy, education, and skilled labor.
- The question is asking about free trade.
- The question is asking about governmental policy implementation.
- The question is asking about aspects of life that influence our happiness.
- The question is asking about the cost of living.

And to question 2:

- The question is asking about job training.
- The question is asking about buying a new car.
- The question is asking about my kids getting summer jobs.
- The question is asking about losing my job.
- The question is asking about my income.
- The question is asking about my income and my wife's.
- The question is asking about me, my wife, and my mother-in-law who lives with us.
- The question is asking about my town where seventy-five people got laid off.
- The question is asking about all the people out of work in my state.

If people interpret the same question so differently, how can their answers be compared or understood by the researchers?

Recently, a member of one of my seminars said she thought we never really think very deeply about the meaning of questions on this kind of survey. We just hear or read the questions and give our responses. She believed that this made the surveys valid. But it doesn't matter how deeply we think about the questions. If we each have different contexts for understanding the question, then our interpretation of its meaning could differ from someone else's. Although researchers perform pre- and posttests of questions that show how a sampling of people understand the questions, they can't know the meaning of everyone's answers without talking to each person.

Organizations need to have some idea of what their clients think of their services or products in order to improve on what they already do and introduce new services or products to the marketplace. But marketing polls, surveys, questionnaires, focus groups (or any other form of consumer research) are not particularly valid unless we can understand the meaning of the customers' responses. We can't do that unless we know how the customers understood the questions they were asked. We can't assume we know that unless we can talk to the customers about it using strategic talk. Labeling research as scientific doesn't negate the fact that all interpretation is based on context. Finding out preferences for one product or service over another requires shared context for understanding.

For example, think of the conversations you've had with people about cars. To really understand why they like one make, dealer, repair shop, style, color, or option over another takes time and talk. You go over it again and again, asking questions, giving examples, telling stories, formulating what's being said or paraphrasing. And then you might begin to understand some preferences that will be meaningful and important to the people who make, sell, and repair cars.

There's no shortcut to understanding the marketplace. Surveys, polls, and questionnaires won't tell you what you need to know until you understand the meaning of the words the way the consumer intended them. To do that, you must make your talk interactive, and you must take an active role in listening and interpreting. In short, you must think of talk as action.

Talking as Action

J. L. Austin, a famous philosopher of language, found it useful to think of some kinds of talk as action. This was a striking thought because it was so different from the standard concepts of words as one thing and actions as another. Austin realized that although words such as *work, study, computer, office, building,* and *machine* are labels for objects and actions in the world, many words aren't. He showed that expressions such as "I promise" are actions in themselves. He called such expressions "speech acts." Speech acts describe utterances in which the words themselves are the actions. For example, if I say, "I promise to deliver the contract tomorrow before lunch," my promising is a speech act. My words are the promising. They aren't a label for a promise out there in the world. In fact, promises can be made only through language.

Promises, requests, offers, commitments, commands, admissions, and declarations are all speech acts that we can use on an everyday basis to do business with associates, customers, and clients. However, we can't use speech acts and assume they're self-explanatory. They aren't. As with any other talk, speech acts are indexical and reflexive. They're not some technical or scientific category of language that is self-evident. They're heard as speech acts because of the context in which they're used, and that context is itself created by our interaction. For example, as Claude is walking over to an important meeting, he runs into Irene, who used to work for his company but now works in a related field in another city. The following conversation ensues:

> *Claude:* Irene! Long time no see.
>
> *Irene:* Claude. It's nice to see you too. How've you been?
>
> *Claude:* Fine. Things are going very well. And with you?
>
> *Irene:* Terrific.
>
> *Claude:* Look, I'm sorry I don't have time to talk just now. I've got this meeting at 10. But what are you doing for lunch tomorrow?
>
> *Irene:* I can't. I'm flying back today. But I promise to call you the next time I'm in town.
>
> *Claude:* Great. I look forward to it. Take care.
>
> *Irene:* You too. Regards to everyone in the office. Bye.
>
> *Claude:* Bye.

Did you hear Irene's promise to call Claude as a real one or simply as the kind of social nicety we've all relied on in similar situations at one time or another? Will Irene call the next time she's in town? To answer these questions, you might want additional information so that you have more context for understanding their conversation. For instance:

- Were Claude and Irene friends before?
- Are they friends now?
- What kind of person is Claude?
- What kind of person is Irene?
- Did they go out to lunch before Irene left the company?
- Do they each make it a practice to go out to lunch with friends and associates?
- Does Irene often make such promises?
- Has she kept them in the past?

These are all relevant questions, and there are others whose answers would help create a context for understanding Irene's promise.

Promises Made

Promises are an important part of doing business. We make promises to meet, to talk, to create, to buy, to sell, to pick up, to deliver. Promises are actions that connect us to people and things in our organization. These connections make things happen. Promises are a kind of talk that creates a link between people and action. Both parties should understand that a promise is a commitment that requires the fulfillment of certain conditions. For example, when a New York computer distributor promises to deliver three computers to a law firm next Friday, that promise is an act in itself. If, next Friday, the computers are delivered, the promise is fulfilled. If the computers don't arrive, there can be trouble, as the following dialogue indicates:

Jack: Where are those computers we ordered?

Phil: Don't worry, you'll have them first thing Monday morning.

Jack: But you promised them this morning.

Phil: Yeah, I know, but we booked a lot of deliveries for today and we can't get to you until next week.

Jack: Then just put them in a cab and send them over this afternoon. We've gotta have them for the weekend.

Phil: Sorry, but our warehouse is in Jersey, we have no one to spare, and we can't get a cabbie to take the responsibility.

Jack: Then we'll send one of our people out there.

Phil: That's fine with me.

Jack: And next time don't make promises you don't intend to keep.

When Phil promised to deliver the computers to Jack's offices, Jack heard him make a commitment to do it. He expected Phil to do what he said he would do. People working on a very important case needed those additional computers that weekend. Jack was angry when Phil didn't fulfill his promise.

We expect others to make only those promises they intend to keep. But promises are not all equal. We don't understand every promise in the same way. Some we take seriously because their fulfillment is very important to us. Some we take less seriously because they aren't so important. And some we don't take seriously at all because they don't matter. As in all cases of understanding, context makes the difference. That's how we recognize a promise as a real promise.

If Phil says, "I will deliver those computers to you on Friday," should Jack hear that as a real promise? How we answer this question affects some important decisions. Should Jack make work plans based on Phil's words? Will Phil structure Friday's delivery schedule to include Jack's firm?

Philosopher John Searle has given us some conditions that are supposed to tell us when to hear particular kinds of talk as real promises. Here's my understanding of those conditions for real promises as applied to Phil and Jack:

1. Phil was not playacting or being sarcastic.
2. Phil promised explicitly to make the delivery.
3. Phil promised to deliver the computers at a specific time.
4. Jack wants Phil to deliver the computers, and Phil believes that Jack wants him to.
5. Phil might not do this otherwise in the normal course of events.
6. Phil intends to make the delivery, and it is within his power to do so.
7. Phil intends the promise to be heard as one.
8. Phil intends Jack to know that making the promise places an obligation on him to deliver the computer on Friday.
9. The rules of English spoken by Phil and Jack make Phil's talk a real promise as long as the preceding eight conditions are fulfilled.

The earlier dialogue makes it clear that Jack heard Phil's talk as a real promise. It also makes it clear that Phil made a promise when he shouldn't have, because he didn't have control over delivery. He might have thought he did, but events that were beyond his control changed that. If we can make real promises only when we have it in our power to do something, then we should never make promises. There is always something that could get in the way of delivering on promises. We could die in the next second. The question then becomes, Is there anything Jack could have done when he bought the computers to make sure that the promise for delivery was real? Could he have used Searle's conditions?

The answer is yes. But not in an automatic way. Like all language, promises are heard in context and are therefore a matter of interpretation. Jack might hear Phil's statement as fulfilling each of the nine conditions. Phil might say that he had every intention of making the delivery on Friday, but he couldn't change the fact that one of his delivery people called in sick. He couldn't fulfill condition 6. Or Phil might say he was actually being sarcastic when he made the promise, so it wasn't a real promise. Condition 1 was missing. Jack misunderstood him.

Promises Kept

It is doubtful that you consciously think about the content of Searle's conditions when you make or hear a promise. But for those situations in which a promise is critical to your operation, you can take the following steps to make sure that a promise is a real promise:

- Remember that Searle's conditions must be interpreted in context.
- Make each detail of fulfillment explicit in conversation and put it in writing.
- Realize that factors that make the fulfillment of any promise possible can change and make it impossible. Therefore, make those factors and their remedy explicit.
- For promises involving future action, constantly monitor what is necessary for their fulfillment. Don't leave the work until the last moment.
- Realize that your understanding of a promise may be different from someone else's. Use paraphrasings, examples, and stories to check agreement.
- Realize that sometimes new promises take precedence over old ones.
- Recognize that most of the time we can't ensure that promises are meant because asking people about their intent questions their integrity.

When someone says, "I promise," it may not mean what you think it means. So if that promise is critical to you, take steps to ensure that it is understood and carried out in a way that is acceptable to you. In order to hear promises, requests, offers, commitments, and all speech acts as the speaker intends, we have to use some version of strategic talk to ensure shared context and understanding. In this way we can use talk to improve business communication for action.

Summary

In this chapter we've looked at talk that makes work happen. We use words to get work done. We depend on them. If we want to get others to act the way we want them to, we have to give them the same resources we have to make the correct practical interpretation. This means talking to them and giving them concrete examples of what we mean.

Anyone who thinks that policies, assignments, rules, directions, orders, and promises won't be misunderstood and misinterpreted had better think again. Misunderstanding may occur because we have to interpret the meaning of the words used. And our interpretation is based on each specific situation. There are no rules for correct interpretation that automatically help us. All language needs to be interpreted. We can prevent misunderstanding only by anticipating it and using the formulations, questions and answers, paraphrasing, examples, and stories of strategic talk.

Use this talk consciously to create and sustain your interpretation of talk. Although talk is not the perfect solution to understanding organizational talk, it seems to be the best solution. In the next chapter, you will see why and how we have to use talk to understand the meaning of the written word, which, although more permanent, can be even more vague and ambiguous than the spoken word.

Chapter Four

Hearing Is Believing:
Talk and the Written Word

The spoken word vanishes, but the written word can come back to haunt us. The written word can get out of control if we don't know how and when to supplement it with talk. Since we have a vested interest in the words we write, we want to be sure people understand what we mean by them. If we do, we can make things happen the way we want them to.

Every Organization Has Its "Bible"

Virtually every organization has some set of written policies or rules that members call the "company bible." It contains information on how some (or all) aspects of the organization ought to work. It may also have a brief history of the organization, how it began, and where it's going.

Imagine that you work in an organization called Creations, Inc., and your bible is the Bible. How clearly would you be able to understand the history, policies and rules of your company? For example, Chapter Two of the Book of Genesis in the King James version of the Old Testament says:

> Thus the heavens and the earth were finished, and all the host of them. And on the seventh day God ended his work which he had made; and he rested on the seventh day from all his work which he had made. . . . And the Lord God formed man of the dust of the ground, and breathed into his nostrils the breath of life; and man became a living soul. . . .

And the Lord God caused a deep sleep to fall upon Adam, and he slept; and he took one of his ribs, and closed up the flesh instead thereof; And the rib, which the Lord God had taken from man, made he a woman, and brought her unto the man.

From our reading, we know that the world was created from the void in six days; that is, 144 hours, or 8,640 minutes. And on the seventh day God rested. Then God created man from dust and woman from man's rib. Will everyone in your company understand this the same way? Back in 1925, your company would have fired John Thomas Scopes because he had a different understanding. He thought creation happened over millions of years as human beings evolved from some common ape-like ancestors.

You might also have trouble with some of the rules. For example, Chapter 25 of the Book of Leviticus says:

And if thy brother be waxen poor, and fallen in decay with thee; then thou shalt relieve him: yea, though he be a stranger, or a sojourner; that he may live with thee. Take thou no usury of him, or increase: but fear thy God; that thy brother may live with thee. Thou shalt not give him thy money upon usury, nor lend him thy victuals for increase.

Does this mean that you can't lend people money and charge them interest? Does it mean that you can't sell your products for more than they cost you? Pretty important questions for your finance and sales divisions. Unfortunately, you have to rely on the text because the CEO of your organization isn't immediately available to clarify what's meant.

Preventing Misunderstandings of the Written Word

How many times have you read a memo or a report and wished the writer were there so you could ask questions about what this or that meant, why the writer said this, what you were really supposed to do as a result of the memo? Chances are you'll have questions, especially when you're not sure you've understood the point or when you doubt the truth or meaning of what's being said. It's frustrating when there's nobody there to ask. The writer explained certain points in the memo or report that you might not have otherwise understood. But some points that you need to know still got left out. And there are always ambiguities that can lead to the wrong interpretation of what's written.

The reality is that all we've learned about spoken language applies equally well to written communication in work situations. Spoken and written communication share the same problems of ambiguity and interpretation. Clear communication of the written word—including job descriptions, performance appraisal systems, books, newspapers, letters, manuals, forms, memos, instructions, questionnaires, and reports—happens through talk.

Most people rely on the written word for critical communication inside and outside the organization. Follow-up discussion doesn't happen until something goes wrong. This is unfortunate because we need talk to clarify written language.

I once gave a seminar on misunderstanding to twenty-five employees from many different areas of Esso Resources. When I started talking about the problems of understanding the written word, one of the managers asked me about the memos he had to depend on. He said he used memos to tell his people what they needed to know about his area of operation. But, he said, his people often misunderstood the real message. What could he do, he asked, to make sure that the people under his management understood his memos? I suggested that the best way was to talk about the memos with the people who had to understand and act on them. He seemed quite annoyed by my answer and replied that he didn't have the time to do that.

The work that we have to do to ensure understanding takes time and effort. This isn't what some people want to hear. In fact, although most people probably believe that we can understand the written word more easily than the spoken word, the opposite is normally true. The written word may seem clearer because it has the advantage of being there to review again; we can't do this with talk unless we have a recording. Nevertheless, if the CEO writes us a memo, she normally won't hand carry it to us and wait to answer our questions about its precise meaning. If she's talking to us in person, or on the phone, she can.

In talk we can remedy ambiguities and other difficulties. Because the speaker and listener are together, the talk can be interactive. The speaker may see puzzlement on the listener's face and explain further. Or the listener may ask questions. But in written language, the writer has the job of making sure that all the information the reader needs to know, but doesn't, is included in writing. No matter how well the writer knows the reader, the ambiguity of language makes this task especially difficult in written language. Unless the reader can talk to the writer, there's no way to clarify misunderstandings. Even so, we trust the written word and tend to rely on it.

When we have information in writing, we know that we can always go back to it and check our memory. If we've come to some contractual agreement with another company or person, we want that agreement in writing to protect us against people's memories. Having it in writing is better than a handshake because a written agreement provides a record that talk does not. It's a tangible piece of hard evidence that ideas were communicated. Signed, written contracts are evidence of what was agreed.

However, written communication doesn't solve the problem of misunderstanding because it can't solve the problems of attention or interpretation. Although written documents are evidence of what was communicated, they don't automatically tell us the meaning of that communication. If we go to court, a written agreement makes better evidence of a deal and its terms than my memory or yours. It's obviously much better than my word against yours. We trust the written word because we can see it, touch it, and read it, and it's there for everybody else to see, touch, and read. The language of contracts is an attempt to be as clear, precise, and unambiguous as we can be in written language. But the courts are filled with cases in which contracts are being disputed, often with arguments latching on a phrase or two that might be interpreted in a variety of ways.

If even specialized language can be misinterpreted, what solutions might there be to misunderstanding? Here we will discuss a number of them, including use of plain language and use of talk to clarify written materials.

Using Plain Language

A movement in the English-speaking world is growing to promote the use of plain language so that people can understand what's important to them without having to learn a specialized language. The plain language movement makes people think about how language makes sense, which is an important step toward understanding how we can achieve clear communication. In that sense, it takes a leadership role in improving the communication process.

A number of influential organizations and professions have joined the push for the use of plain language, rather than jargon, in their writing for people outside their field. Representatives of government, business, and the legal profession from the United States, Canada, England, New Zealand, Australia, and Hong Kong attended a recent meeting on plain language held in Vancouver, British Columbia.

The plain language movement argues that everybody who has to sign or use contracts, warnings, directions, tax returns, agreements, manuals, and other important written material should be able to understand the meaning of the document without extensive training. For example, the language of an old real estate listing contract read:

> The owner irrevocably assigns to the listing agent and to
> such sub-agent hereby entitled to a portion thereof a suffi-
> cient amount of the purchase price of the property to pay the
> commission and the owner hereby directs and authorizes his
> solicitors to pay the same to the listing agent or sub-agent
> hereby entitled to a portion thereof on or before the third

business day after the adjustment date or the possession date (whichever is the earlier day) for the sale, lease or for the exchange.

The new contract says:

> You'll pay the real estate commission to the listing agent no later than the second business day after the sale is completed, unless you and the listing agent otherwise agree in writing. A sale is completed when the change of ownership is registered with the Land Titles Office and the buyer pays the purchase money.

Undoubtedly we can simplify written language. However, this leaves the problem of ambiguity unresolved. Those in the plain language movement seem not to recognize the importance of interpretation and context. Will this new wording lead to less litigation over contracts? Certainly the language *seems* easier to understand. But is it? It may in fact turn out to be more ambiguous than before because it's less technical. The jargon of law has more precise meaning for those who have been trained to understand it. Plain language presents more ambiguity because it has a wider range of contextual possibilities. People may also assume they share understanding and ask fewer questions about correct interpretation. As a result, trying to cut down on litigation by making the language simpler may have exactly the reverse effect. So, if plain language isn't a surefire solution, we're back to relying on talk to clarify the written language we do use.

Clarifying Correspondence, Memos, and Reports with Talk

Your knowledge of indexicality and reflexivity and their relationship to misunderstanding might appear to make clear communication much easier. However, the nature of language hasn't changed. You're just conscious of the cause of the difficulties that language creates. We can make letters and memos communicate what we want them to communicate if we're willing to take the time and energy to do it. That means we can no longer use letters or memos the way most of us have.

We can, however, use some shortcuts. Say, for example, that I'm manager of production and that employees' understanding of my memo on new product development is critical. I don't have time to talk to everyone concerned so I plan meetings with my department heads to talk about the memo. They ask questions and get clarification from me, and I ask them to tell me how they understand what I've written. They can then discuss it in the same way at meetings with people in their departments. Everyone gets a chance to talk about it with someone who has discussed it with me. And since I wrote it, I'm the authority. I will also ensure that I'm available in person, or by phone, or on electronic mail, to discuss it with anyone who still has questions or comments about its meaning. The more critical the communication, the more important the talk about it.

Dorothy Winsor has written extensively about some memo trouble that came to light during an investigation of the *Challenger* space shuttle disaster. I've chosen this particular example because of the serious consequences of the misunderstanding involved. Here are two memos on the same subject. The first is the full text of an internal memo from a Morton Thiokol International (MTI) engineer to the MTI vice president of engineering:

> This letter is written to insure that management is fully aware of the seriousness of the current O-ring erosion problem in the SRM joints from an engineering standpoint. The mistakenly accepted position on the joint problem was to fly without fear of failure and to run a series of design evaluations which would ultimately lead to a solution or at least a significant reduction of the erosion problem. This position is now drastically changed as a result of the SRM 16A nozzle joint erosion which eroded a secondary O-ring with the primary O-ring never sealing.
>
> If the same scenario should occur in a field joint (and it could), then it's a jump ball as to the success or failure of the

joint because the secondary O-ring can't respond to the clevis opening rate and may not be capable of pressurization. The result would be a catastrophe of the highest order—loss of human life. An unofficial team [a memo defining the team and its purpose was never published] with the leader was formed on 19 July 1985 and was tasked with solving the problem for both the short and long term. This unofficial team is essentially nonexistent at this time. In my opinion, the team must be officially given the responsibility and the authority to execute the work that needs to be done on a non-interference basis (full time assignment until completed).

It's my honest and very real fear that if we don't take immediate action to dedicate a team to solve the problem with the field joint having the number one priority, then we stand in jeopardy of losing a flight along with all the launch pad facilities.

We must understand MTI management's interpretation of this memo in light of the knowledge that MTI engineering personnel, including the author of the memo, had, until this time, supported continued work toward launching the shuttle because they believed the secondary O-rings would seal in the event of primary O-ring failure despite some evidence to the contrary.

Compare this memo to one, on the same subject, from another MTI engineer to an official at the Marshall Space Center, headquarters of the shuttle program, about the effect of cold temperatures on the O-rings:

Subject: Actions Pertaining to the SRM Field Joint Secondary Seal. Per your request, this letter contains the answers to the two questions you asked at the July Problem Review Board telecon.

1. *Question:* If the field joint secondary seal lifts off the metal mating surfaces during motor pressurization, how soon will it return to a position where contact is re-established?

Answer: Bench test data indicate that the o-ring resiliency (its capability to follow the metal) is a function of temperature and the rate of case expansion. MTI measured the force of the o-ring against Instron plattens, which simulated the nominal squeeze on the o-ring and approximated the case expansion distance and rate. At 100°F the o-ring maintained contact. At 75°F the o-ring lost contact for 2.4 seconds. At 50°F the o-ring didn't re-establish contact in ten minutes at which time the test was terminated. The conclusion is that secondary sealing capability in the SRM field joint can't be guaranteed.

2. *Question:* If the primary o-ring doesn't seal, will the secondary seal seat in sufficient time to prevent joint leakage?

Answer: MTI has no reason to suspect that the primary seal would ever fail after pressure equilibrium is reached, i.e., after the ignition transient. If the primary o-ring were to fail from 0 to 170 milliseconds, there's a very high probability that the secondary o-ring would hold pressure since the case hasn't expanded appreciably at this point. If the primary seal were to fail from 170 to 330 milliseconds, the probability of the secondary seal holding is reduced. From 330 to 660 milliseconds the chance of the secondary seal holding is small. This is a direct result of the o-ring's slow response compared to the metal case segments as the joint rotates.

Please call me or Mr. Roger Boisjoly if you have additional questions concerning this issue.

The first memo never went outside MTI. The engineer who wrote it marked it "Company Private." Reading it, one might ask how the message it was sending could be misunderstood. Nevertheless, management's understanding of the problem allowed them to give less importance to the memo than we do as outsiders. For whatever reason, they didn't see it as good reason to stop the launch.

The second memo went from MTI to Marshall. There it was passed on to the solid rocket booster project manager who was to send it to NASA. He vetoed that, saying the information in the memo was "old news." At the shuttle disaster investigation, this manager said he had not realized the memo's significance. "There were a whole lot of people who weren't smart enough to look behind the veil and say, 'Gee, I wonder what this means.'"

At the shuttle disaster investigation, the NASA official who was to have received the memo said, "I don't know if anybody at that time understood the joint well enough to realize that the data was crucial." Remember that we're talking about misunderstanding a memo that was sent by one engineer to another engineer, both of whom were working on the same project. What better evidence of the problems of interpretation that exist in written communication? Dorothy Winsor, who wrote the analysis from which this example is drawn, sums up the problem of understanding when she says, "That this memo didn't communicate its intent is shown by the fact that the people who read it were uncertain about what it meant."

Correspondence, memos, and reports containing critical information have to be discussed by the people who write them and the people who have to understand and act on them. We should never assume that letters, memos, or reports can be adequately understood by others simply by reading them. This isn't because we can't read or write well but rather because of the nature of language and its connection to misunderstanding.

Some organizations might call such explications a waste of time and money. And for noncritical situations, they may be right. But we know from our experience and from our knowledge of how language works that written language has more problems of understanding than spoken language. So in critical situations, these steps are absolutely necessary.

Clarifying Written Instructions

Have you ever tried to put toys together on Christmas Eve, after your children have gone to bed? You were tired yourself and would rather have been in bed, but instead you had to try to understand exactly what step A entailed and why this screw wouldn't fit in that hole. The instructions for doing the job seemed to have been written by someone who had already put the toy together a hundred times. If only the person had been there so you could ask questions.

Many of us have also faced problems with learning how to use computers by reading the manuals. Companies have recognized the dilemma and offer toll-free customer support numbers. For example, WordPerfect gives this option: "If you need assistance beyond what the manual, the Help feature, and your dealer can provide . . . toll-free support is available by dialing. . . ." When was the last time you didn't need any help?

Organizations other than computer companies have also begun toll-free lines for customers to use for help. Instructions for using any complicated machine need to be augmented by talk between those who know how to use the machines and those who don't. This can often be accomplished through training. If that isn't possible because of unit costs, then telephone hotlines are a good substitute. In putting together toys and equipment, you may have been helped by a less expensive alternative: a drawing or picture that made the job much easier. Drawings and pictures are analogous to the concrete examples in talk.

Remember that the principal problems of understanding written instructions come from the nature of language rather than the writer. But clearly, the problems of language affect us all.

Making Job Descriptions Work

An organization had a serious problem with new employees. When they were evaluated at the end of their six-month probationary period, many of them complained that they were being evaluated on tasks and responsibilities that weren't part of their written job descriptions. The supervisors felt they understood the jobs to be done and that the descriptions were more than adequate.

The problem turned out to be one of context. The supervisors had a context for understanding the written descriptions that the new employees could not possibly share. The supervisors had been with the organization for a long time and had done those jobs. They knew where those jobs fit in the entire work of the division. They also understood what separated outstanding work from average and poor work. This quality was hard to put into a job description because it involved personal traits such as attitude, dedication, flexibility, creativity, and going that extra mile.

But the new employees had a context also, and that was not shared by the supervisors. The jobs had changed since the supervisors had done them. There were new ways of doing things, new people to work with, new technology and new policies, goals and attitudes within the organization that affected the job. The supervisors didn't understand these differences. From the supervisor's point of view, an employee was responsible for getting the job done in the manner the supervisor expected. The new employee had to learn these expectations, which was not always easy because the supervisor took most of the expectations for granted. Then the supervisor criticized the employee for not having done what was never made explicit in the first place. The employees and supervisors had different interpretations of the job description. Each had a different context for understanding the meanings of the words. Here's one approach to solving this kind of problem.

Everyone has to learn to think about what *counts* as the job, not what *is* the job. This is a far more realistic way of thinking about job descriptions. It says that doing the job means doing what the people you report to expect you to do. This meaning of the job often doesn't get spelled out in explicit detail in job descriptions. It happens when the supervisor and employee create a shared context for understanding how the job should be done. Sometimes this doesn't happen because people don't realize that it needs to. They think that formal written job descriptions are comprehensive and accurate. Using what we understand about the indexicality of language we know that job descriptions can have many different meanings depending on the context that the reader provides. With this knowledge as a starting point, we can change the way we write job descriptions.

Here are three basic steps to follow to build a custom-made job description around a basic core:

1. Give examples. To the basic job description, add examples of what counts as the job. These examples should come out of discussions between the supervisor and the employee.

2. Revise descriptions as part of each review. Supervisor and employee should review the job description at least once each year and add or delete descriptions and examples to reflect changes in the job and changes in the competencies of the employee over time.

3. Combine the job description with the performance appraisal. This helps ensure that the employee and supervisor both have the same context for what counts as doing the job.

These steps customize the descriptions and ensure that they are discussed and revised with some frequency.

A Better Answer: Monday Notes

An excellent way to use written communication to ensure understanding is to make it interactive. The famous rocket scientist, Wernher von Braun, was appointed director of the Marshall Space Flight Center in 1960. As Phillip Tompkins has reported, in order to keep up with what was happening with the nearly two dozen lab directors and program managers, von Braun asked each of them to send him a weekly, one-page note summarizing the progress and problems of the week. He purposely refused to design some form for the directors and managers to fill out. All he wanted was a name and a date and their one-page commentary. The notes were due in the director's office each Monday.

These Monday notes proved a successful way for people to communicate directly to management and to each other. Von

Braun initialed and dated each report as he read it and made extensive comments in the margins for later discussion: questions, suggestions, and compliments for jobs well done. Monday notes from all the managers, together with von Braun's marginal annotations, were copied and sent to all the contributors.

The value of the Monday notes was clear. They kept the director informed. They let everyone know what was going on in everyone else's shop. They were not the end product of communication but the beginning. They gave people feedback on their own work as well as that of their associates. Communication within labs was improved because the lab directors prepared their Monday notes based on information passed on to them by their subordinates. Notes from different labs often discussed the same problem, and this redundancy ensured that no critical information was lost or ignored. The notes went directly from the working labs to the director and could not be blocked, edited, or changed in any way by the layer of management between the labs and von Braun.

This informal and regular exchange of information, ideas, opinions, problems, and solutions formed the basis for further communication between people about common problems and progress. The notes were the foundation for a shared context for understanding what people were doing and what they were writing and talking about at their work. People at Marshall said they liked the personalized nature of the notes. Compared to most of the formal and sterile communication they sent or received, these were informal, quick, and wonderfully human. People saw themselves and others as real people in those notes. Sometimes managers used the notes to carry on arguments with other managers; as they put it, "We sometimes misuse them—to get attention."

These notes were the most effective kind of written reports because they were essentially interactive. Their frequency, the immediate response of the director, and their circulation among all contributors resulted in a form of written conversation that led spontaneously to spoken conversation on issues of critical importance to any of the participants. The notes depended on and also contributed to building a common stock of knowledge among the readers. This common stock of knowledge created a shared context for understanding.

It's hard to imagine many large organizations, especially those with any government affiliation, tolerating an informal, written communication system like this that purposely bypasses certain levels of the management hierarchy. Downward directed communication remains the preferred style. For example, in 1967, NASA asked all its field centers to put in place their own system of Monday notes. But ignoring the informality, simplicity, and open-endedness that made von Braun's system so successful, they sent each center a volume of directions on how to do it, including numbered forms to be used for the notes. They had not realized what made this particular type of written communication work.

I've recently had the chance to test Monday notes in another setting. Peter Graves, marketing manager at the local office of Worldwide Travel, a large and growing travel consortium, wanted to improve ways of exchanging information and ideas and keeping up-to-date with his travel consultants. I suggested he try using Monday notes to keep in touch with his people, their ideas, and their problems and feelings about their work, clients, and the company. In a letter to me, dated January 8, 1993, he wrote the following:

> [O]ur Monday notes program is continuing to be successful. It has been an excellent forum for everyone here to express their ideas and concerns.
>
> The program has been a true asset to me, as we continue to slash through the challenges of becoming the nation's undisputed leading travel management company.

Monday notes are one method for improved communication, and one that has seen the test of time. But what of newer methods for communication, ones that are linked to advances in the electronic age?

E-Mail and Other Human-Machine Communication

Many of us today use computers to communicate with our associates. Our machines transmit written communication that isn't face-to-face yet is interactive, that isn't oral yet differs from normal writing; that isn't regular mail yet is written; that isn't conversation, yet people take turns. We use E-mail, computer conferencing, and fax machines where we would have used letters, memos, the telephone, or face-to-face meetings. These methods are speedy but warrant a warning: machines that generate, store, and communicate information mask the interpretive process that creates and makes sense of information. We must therefore be aware of how they can change our understanding of what's communicated.

Are there any guidelines for using these new technologies to communicate effectively? These are evolving as the technologies do and within the organizations that use them. For instance, after employees at my publisher used E-mail in-house for some time, they came up with working guidelines concerning what should and should not be communicated and discussed via E-mail. As one example, they found that E-mail, as they were using it, was not an efficient way to schedule meetings and develop agenda. It seemed as though it would be: everyone concerned received immediate notification of a planned meeting and a tentative agenda; each team member could then commit to coming to the meeting or suggest a different time and date; everyone concerned had an opportunity to provide input as to what would be discussed. But amid these responses (copies of which every participant received), the purpose of the original notice sometimes got jumbled. People lost sight of who had called the meeting in the first place and why. After living with this snowball effect for a while, they revised how E-mail is to be used in planning meetings. The person calling the meeting sends out an announcement via E-mail to all participants. People can then use E-mail to acknowledge the meeting and commit to coming. But anyone who can't make the meeting or who has a suggestion for the agenda must take it up with the sender, face-to-face.

Although machine-mediated communication may not always be the best or most appropriate way of communicating, E-mail, computer conferencing, and networking do enjoy many of the advantages of conversation and writing. They are more interactive than standard correspondence and produce records of what was "said" in a way that spoken conversations don't (unless they are recorded). Anyone who has something to say can do so and can take a turn at any time. The computer will display new input at the next available time.

Some research I did on the subject of computer conferencing showed that it was a definite improvement over traditional written communication because the computer programs used controlled, and made explicit, certain important features needed to produce coherent and understandable "talk," such as topic formulation and personal biographies of the participants.

The disadvantages of this type of communication include the fact that it requires learning a new etiquette so you can say what you want to say electronically and still maintain good social relations with the participants. How do you interact with people when you can't see them or hear them? Normal contextual and nonverbal cues are absent, so it's more difficult to interpret meaning. And unless the system is on-line, there may not be immediate feedback on questions of understanding and interpretation.

Computer-generated written communication does have its advantages. It can be stored and read at a convenient time. Depending on oral communication can be risky in certain circumstances if the speaker or listener can't pay proper attention to the message. When lives are at risk, this consideration can become very important.

Relying on Communication Links

The Federal Aviation Administration (FAA) has decided to lessen the chances of misunderstanding between air traffic controllers (ATCs) and pilots by using new procedures for transmitting airline predeparture clearances (PDCs). The new system will replace lengthy, error-prone, cockpit-tower voice communications with a data link to hard-copy printers in the cockpit. The FAA associate administrator says this technique should eliminate more than 50 percent of the human errors involving altitude assignment and radio frequency changes.

With this new system, the flight crew uses a push-button controller to make a PDC request that is ultimately transmitted from the airline's computer to the control tower. The tower sends the PDC to the aircraft via an electronic data link, which effectively prevents misunderstanding due to mishearing. However, voice contact remains essential as a means of preventing misinterpretations due to the nature of the language used. The specialized jargon of ATC reduces the ambiguity inherent in language, but because of the contextual basis of meaning, it doesn't eliminate it completely. Talk between tower and aircraft can't be totally eliminated because the ATC instructions must take account of the individual needs of the plane and its crew.

In spite of these problems, any system that increases interactive written communication is an improvement. Nevertheless, such a system isn't a substitute for talk. This fact becomes more obvious when we consider other kinds of electronic communication.

Maintaining Records and Accuracy

Medical charts in hospitals are now more and more likely to be generated electronically. No more do the nurse and the doctor scribble indecipherable remarks on a clipboard kept at the foot of the patient's bed. Instead, computers keep track of records. Automated charting systems capture, store, retrieve, and present patients' clinical files. Computers collect data automatically from medical devices and store it. The data can then be presented in formats useful to nurses, doctors, and therapists.

Using machines that generate, store, and communicate information might seem like a good way to avoid misunderstanding caused by people needing to interpret language. Automated charts are clear and legible. Many may seem less open to misunderstanding than a written order or a nurse's note. And they can reduce the amount of time nurses spend verifying chart contents. But they can't eliminate interpretation of written language.

The data get into the computer by way of computer software that someone wrote. The software tells the machine how to identify and interpret certain kinds of information. This information gets printed on charts in various formats that someone designed. The data then get read and interpreted in the same way as any other written document is interpreted. Electronically creating written documents merely substitutes the software writer's interpretation of data and language for the technician's. It doesn't eliminate the need for the nurse, physician, or therapist to make sense of the charts. Another downside is that having records made electronically can decrease the amount of time the doctor actually spends bedside, therefore decreasing the potential for communication between patient and doctor and patient's family and doctor.

Beware of claims that we can do away with interpretation for creating or presenting written data. Such claims usually ignore the importance of context in making sense of communications.

Summary

Making written communication work for you means recognizing the problems of written language and knowing the solutions. The problems with written communication include the following:

- Written language is just as ambiguous as spoken language.
- Written language, like spoken language, gets its meaning from our interpretation of it.
- Written language needs shared context for understanding.
- Writers must write for an imagined audience; unfortunately, the actual audience may not have the background knowledge and expertise that the writer anticipated.
- Writers are not always available to clarify their writing.
- Lengthy written communication probably will not be read by the intended audience.

The solutions to these problems come from what we know about misunderstanding:

- Realize that your written words probably will not be understood by your audience exactly as you intended.
- Know that the larger your audience, the greater the chance of misunderstanding.
- Ask yourself what you *think* the readers know and what you *know* they know about the subject of your document.
- Ask yourself what other resources the readers have for understanding.
- Provide those resources the readers need but don't have.
- Never assume that written communication is self-explanatory.
- Keep your written communications brief and to the point.
- Make written communication interactive by being available to talk about what you write.
- Encourage feedback by structuring it into your communication.
- Don't make people write important information in some preset form.
- Require face-to-face meetings on all important documents with the people who must act on them.

The bottom line on written communication is that we have to plan follow-up talk on critical written communication as part of our normal way of doing business. Minutes spent in talking now will save hours, days, or even weeks spent in trying to clear up misunderstandings later on. These savings translate directly to the bottom line in terms of time, travel, legal fees, goodwill, and referrals.

Chapter Five

Differences That Make a Difference: Talking Across Stereotypes

We live in an age during which groups of all kinds are talking about their identity and rights. Every day we hear about some new group in the workplace claiming, often with complete justification, that they should be consulted about an issue that concerns them. At the same time that people across the world seem to coming together, many people are choosing to emphasize their special group identity rather than other possible identities. This assertion of group identity has created a new sensitivity to cross-cultural and cross-gender communication.

This chapter recasts the notion of group identity regarding issues of communication. Instead of emphasizing the need to be sensitive to gender and ethnic differences, it extends the earlier discussion to show that using gender and cultural stereotypes can contribute to misunderstanding by oversimplifying the issue of shared context. Talking to people simply as representatives of their gender or ethnic group ignores or obscures the difficulty we always face in creating shared context for understanding. Group and gender identity can be very significant aspects of context, but they're not automatically significant. Within our own gender or group, we can often experience misunderstanding because of an assumed but absent shared context.

Gender and ethnic labels won't succeed as shortcuts to understanding. Instead, clear communication depends on talking to people as individuals rather than as members of groups; shared context, whatever it turns out to be, has to be worked out and established in each individual interaction with others. Above all, knowing someone's group identity doesn't give us a script to use in talking to them. We and they must still make sense of each other using whatever is appropriate to the situation, including what arises in the situation itself. This chapter should provide you with a new understanding of our individual responsibility for making sense of each other that depends more on knowing how language works than on our stereotypes of group identity.

Do You Know a Stereotype?

"You know what they're like."

"Yeah. They're all the same. They don't have a sense of humor. And they don't understand our way of doing things."

"They're all so calm; it's amazing to me."

"I know, and they're really hard workers. They often work two or three jobs, just to earn enough to open their own business."

Everyone reading this book has heard positive and disparaging remarks made about some group or other. For many of us, a single word—*women, men, blacks, whites, Jews, Italians, Californians, Southerners*—paints some picture in our minds. But how useful is this picture?

Every day we interact with people of the opposite sex or different backgrounds. Our associates and employees are increasingly likely to be a mixed lot. An article by Jolie Solomon in the *Wall Street Journal* reports that white males will make up less than 40 percent of the United States labor force by the year 2000. Increasing their numbers will be women and people of African, Hispanic, Asian, and Native American origin. How do we cope with the gender, ethnic, cultural, religious, racial, linguistic, and other differences of those in our organization and other people with whom we associate? We might seem to speak the same language, but how do we cope with the differences in meaning that come from upbringing, accent, habits, expectations, ethics, motives, customs, desires, likes, dislikes, prejudices, and background?

It may all seem too overwhelming. Nevertheless, we have to be sensitive to people who are different, or we may lose our jobs or businesses. We need to know the significant differences and similarities to find a common ground for clear communication. For most of us, however, the problem isn't how to talk to people of other cultures or the opposite gender but how to talk with one person in particular, with the individuals with whom we have to do business.

Determining Groups

Harry M. Johnson, in his introduction to sociology, points out that our choice to identify people as members of social groups is arbitrary because to do so is to emphasize one aspect of their identity at the expense of others. We all have many group memberships, each of which accents some aspect of our identity. But we can be a member of many other groups besides. For example, one person can be businessperson, owner, employee, marketing expert, craftsperson, lawyer, female, wife, golfer, tennis player, black, American, Californian, Republican, tall, good-looking, mother, grandmother, and so on. It's easy to see that some of these identities don't necessarily require any other, even though some may go together. A businessperson may have none, some, or all of the factors listed.

On this basis, we can say that the differences among people within groups can be greater than differences between groups. The differences among females can be greater than the differences between females and males. The differences among males can be greater than the differences between males and females. The differences among blacks can be greater than the differences between blacks and whites. As a consequence, when we talk to people, we can't rely on generalizations about their group identity or gender to tell us what they're like as individuals and what specific context they're going to use to interpret what we say to them. We can only work that out in our interaction with them. We can use cultural background or gender as a potentially useful bit of context for understanding but certainly not as a script to tell us how to talk to all people of a particular background or gender.

This is not an ethical or moral argument against stereotyping, although such an argument could certainly be made. It's a question of economy and utility. Misunderstanding in organizations normally wastes time and money. To minimize this waste we need a shared context for understanding in each situation. We can't depend on stereotypes to do the job: individuals may or may not share the stereotypical characteristics of their group.

Participants in my seminars on critical communication perform an exercise to start them thinking about social stereotypes. They think of a specific, identifiable racial, cultural, ethnic, religious, or gender group different from their own. They list the most obvious and defining characteristics of members of that group. They do this by answering the question, What are they really like? Then they think of their own gender or racial, cultural, ethnic, or religious group. They list the most obvious and defining characteristics of that group. Again, they answer the question, What are they really like?

Then they compare and contrast the similarities and differences between the groups and give specific examples of behavior to illustrate their lists of characteristics. This is where the trouble begins. Their examples create problems. Participants frequently disagree on what the behavior described in the examples really shows. They bicker about the meaning of the behavior. They also argue about how typical it is of the group in question. In most cases, the generalizations begin to self-destruct as soon as the participants talk about real people in real situations.

Generalizing to Make Sense of the World

We need to make our very complex world a manageable place to live. How we actually do this has been postulated in many theories. One theory says that as infants we see the world as one huge mass of experiences with little to distinguish one event from another, one object from another. As we grow up we learn language. We use language to reduce the vast number of different stimuli in the world to manageable size by using words for categories of apparently similar things. We give names to groups of beings and objects, such as bird, chair, woman, man, book, bank, blue, boss, employee, car, by emphasizing their common traits and ignoring their specific, individual characteristics.

Take the word *bird*, for example. It includes small birds (sparrows) and big birds (condors); birds that fly a lot (crows), a little (chickens), and not at all (ostriches); birds that can fly forward, backward, and that can hover (hummingbirds); birds that swim on top of the water (ducks); birds that dive and swim under the water (cormorants); birds that eat seeds (pigeons), worms (robins), insects (swallows), other birds (falcons), mammals (hawks), fish (penguins), and almost anything (magpies); birds that migrate (terns) and birds that don't (quail); birds that we hunt (pheasants) and birds that we don't (eagles). The list of differences could continue for pages. So saying "Look at the bird" tells us very little about an individual bird, except that it is within view.

Generalizing makes it possible for us to communicate with each other about the world. Imagine what language would be like if each word had to completely capture the uniqueness of the object or event it was to describe. Generalizing gives us a language and a world that are manageable. But it also distorts the world. The world and our language can be said to mutually create each other; that is, we can have many different versions of the world depending on how we describe it. This accounts for the variety in eyewitness accounts of the same event. Can we give the one and only true account? Only when we're able to stand outside our human condition and use language that doesn't include our own experience, prejudices, likes and dislikes, and practical interests. That's something we can't do.

There's another useful way to think about the inherent problem of stereotyping and generalization. Ludwig Wittgenstein, a famous twentieth-century philosopher of language who taught at Oxford University, recognized that we would have great difficulty trying to describe the objects and activities of the world precisely using our language. Things in the world, including our descriptions of them, exhibit what Wittgenstein called "family resemblances." We can recognize things that go together in the same way that we can see that members of an extended family share a shape or size of nose, or hair color, or physique, or shape and color of eyes. Not everyone in the family shares the same trait with everyone else, and members at the opposite ends of the family line may share no obvious traits. But each shares at least one trait with at least one other member. We can often pick out family members using these resemblances. However, we can't predict what some unseen member of the extended family will look like. We have to see that member to know whom he or she resembles.

Obviously we lose a lot of information about people and objects when we generalize. But it often may not make any difference. If your boss asks you to put another chair around the boardroom table, and you say, "Exactly what kind of chair did you want? A folding chair, an armchair, a wing chair, a reclining chair, a wooden chair, a leather chair, an antique chair, a swivel chair, a rocking chair?" you might get a very strange look. You're expected to use your common sense to find a suitable chair.

But generalizations can also have pernicious consequences, as even a quick scan of the news tells us. Northern Ireland, the Middle East, Yugoslavia, the former Soviet Union, Germany, North Africa, South Africa, Los Angeles, and New York are just a few of the many places where people use racial, religious, ethnic, linguistic and cultural generalizations to justify killing each other.

We do need to generalize in order to cope with the world, but we also have to look carefully at the evidence in support of many generalizations about people. Upon examination, the generalizations may turn out to be no more than useful fictions in the sense that the evidence wouldn't stand up to rigorous scrutiny. If we believe that our generalizations about people are true, we can be sacrificing just the kind of flexibility that successful communication demands.

In an article on cross-cultural management, Rose Knotts stresses the importance of flexibility and sincerity in intercultural situations. She says that to avoid mistakes and misunderstandings in managing intercultural relationships, we must develop an awareness of the other culture's habits, actions, and reasons for behavior.

No one can deny that flexibility, sincerity, and awareness of others are very important traits for managers to have. But this has to do with our interaction with individuals, not cultures. We do belong to cultures, and we do have gender identities. But understanding group habits, actions, and reasons for behavior in the abstract is different from understanding why Yasuko Shibayama, Jose Gonzales, Denzel Jones, or Elizabeth Brown say what they say and do what they do. We have to recognize that communication is ultimately a problem between individuals. When you or I listen or talk, read or write, it's not our group doing it—it's you or me, with whatever family resemblances we may have from the groups of which we're members. The resemblances that may appear in our talk and behavior aren't predetermined; whatever may be true about our group may not be true about you or me as individual members of that group. Perhaps the most freely discussed group differences surround gender; in the next section, we discuss some of the generalizations we make about women and men.

Going Beyond Gender Generalizations

Generalizations about the differences between women and men are supported by research on differences between female and male talk. Communication researchers Nancy Henley and Cheris Kramarae have written extensively on gender differences in language use. These different languages reflect both the intrinsic differences between genders as well as learned differences.

The most widely accepted theory of female-male difference is called the two cultures theory. It says the problem of miscommunication between women and men comes from the fact that they live in two different worlds. Girls grow up with experiences quite different from boys. These experiences come from a female approach to social relationships that emphasizes cooperation and equality. Girls invest in close friendships in which they share all their important growing-up experiences. Girls learn to be sensitive to relationships and social situations. Boys, on the other hand, experience a world of power and control. They strive to dominate people and situations. They seek to establish and maintain their individual identities. Boys agree and disagree, argue and compete. Girls learn to use language to maintain social relationships. Boys learn to use language as a form of verbal aggression. Gender differences in conversational style reflect different ways of seeing the world. As a result of these different experiences, women and men use language in ways that are so different that misunderstanding is inevitable.

This theory has found its most popular expression in Deborah Tannen's book, aptly titled *You Just Don't Understand: Conversations Between Men and Women*. Many women who've read Tannen's book identify with it completely. Men and women alike say it picks up the differences very accurately. But even after reading it, they don't know what to do about these differences in their own interactions with the opposite sex.

It's often difficult to apply generalizations about the social world to our own experience. Generalizations can't capture the uniqueness of our individual experience interacting with others, nor is it claimed that they can. Gender differences may or may not be relevant to communicating a particular thought. What do the biological differences between men and women mean when women and men are talking to one another? It might depend on the subject. Some misunderstanding between the sexes may be the result of biological differences and how they affect life experiences. However, topics affected by these differences—childbirth, disease, and maturation—are few. And even gender differences aren't always clear-cut or apparent. To use the fact that women and men are biologically different and have different reproductive functions is fraught with problems. To generalize about women and men's context for understanding talk in a one-on-one situation prevents clear communication, for a variety of reasons.

If you follow sports, you may know that Stella Walsh was the dominant women's sprinter during the 1930s and 1940s. Born in Poland in 1911, she moved with her parents to the United States just before World War I and changed her name from Stanislowa Walasiewicz. She won the gold medal in the 100 meters in the 1932 Los Angeles Olympics and the silver in the Berlin Games of 1936.

According to an Associated Press story out of New Orleans, on December 9, 1980, Stella Walsh was shot to death in an attempted armed robbery. Then the controversy began. A coroner's report said she had ambiguous genitalia; she had a condition known as "mosaicism," which means she had both male and female characteristics. Analysis of her chromosomes showed that she had a majority of typically male chromosomes in her cells. Was she a man or a woman? If she was a woman, then she deserves to keep all of her many track medals and records. If she was a man, she should lose them. What would you say? Was she male or female?

Perhaps you'd base your decision on whether Stella did or could have borne children. But many women with standard chromosomal configurations can't have children. To complicate matters further, there are cases on record in which women found to have a majority of male chromosomes later bore children. And there are other cases of prepubescent girls who are physically female but hormonally male. How would you talk with one of these people? Would you talk as though you were talking to a woman or to a man? Would knowledge of someone's chromosomes make a difference in your talk?

Consider Allan, who spent the early hours of a Christmas party talking to a very attractive woman. She was tall, had long blonde hair, a rather deep voice, and a beautiful complexion. Later on, Allan's friend Jacquie asked if he knew whom he'd been talking to. Not really, he said, since he'd just met her this evening. Jacquie told Allan that the "she" used to be a "he." If Allan had known this before, how might the conversation have differed? There would have been differences, of course, but they would have come out of a highly complex interaction, not the result of an automatic script for talking to men who had undergone a sex change and were now women.

In the movies, passing for the opposite gender creates many wonderful and entertaining situations. In "Some Like It Hot," Tony Curtis and Jack Lemmon pretend to be female musicians. In "Victor Victoria," Julie Andrews plays a woman pretending to be a man pretending to be a woman. In "Tootsie," Dustin Hoffman plays a very convincing woman. And in "La Cage Aux Folles," some male show-girls are every bit as beautiful as the females. We don't know which is which until the men take off their wigs at the end of the show.

The issue of male/female equivocality raises interesting questions about the reality of gender identity as a dependable guide to shared context. We know someone's gender only after the clothes are off. And even then we can't always be absolutely sure. So, since we can't be certain, we must learn to take each interaction as it comes. If we rely on stereotypes to tell us how to communicate, clear communication will be difficult, if not impossible.

We can use general notions of female/male differences when we realize that the many problems of misunderstanding between men and women are based on the same basic features of talk that underlie misunderstanding between all people: the problem of multiple meanings in language and the absence of shared context. Women and men also misunderstand each other for the same reasons women misunderstand women and men misunderstand men. The nature of language itself causes misunderstanding. We can know how we understand what someone says, but we have to work at seeing if that's what they intended us to understand.

When Misunderstanding Becomes Sexual Harassment

To put the problems of female-male communication, misunderstanding, and gender stereotyping in perspective we need to look at real-life situations. What should we do if an associate at work persistently comes on to us? How do we make that person understand that the attention is unwanted? Do men and women speak the same language? Should they?

Sexual harassment can be a conscious and deliberate verbal or physical assault. It can, however, be less malicious and result from misunderstanding, perhaps gender miscommunication. Millions of people were glued to their TV sets during the Senate hearings over Clarence Thomas's nomination to the U.S. Supreme Court. Anita Hill, a law professor and former employee of Thomas, complained that he'd harassed her over ten years previously when she worked with him in Washington. She described Thomas as a boss who continually pestered her for dates and spoke to her about pornography, bestiality, rape, and his own sexual prowess. Asking for dates or discussing such topics aren't in themselves sexual harassment. But doing so after the other person has explicitly said that she is not interested can be.

In situations like this, harassment can result from misunderstanding: when we think we're making ourselves clear but we're not understood the way we intend. Depending on the evidence from the talk and its context, we can say the misunderstanding was reasonable or unreasonable. When the talk shows that a man holds certain stereotypical views of women such that he doesn't understand a woman's explicit message to stop the way she intends, that misunderstanding is unreasonable.

Thomas categorically denied that he ever did or said what Hill alleged. Since the incidents were said to have happened over ten years earlier, it was Thomas's word against Hill's. The Senate Committee, fourteen men, voted to confirm Thomas's appointment. In the issue of *Newsweek* that discussed the Hill/Thomas case, a follow-up article (by Kaplan, McDaniel, and Anin) on sexual harassment gave the following example. Saying "Hey, great legs" to someone at work is harassment; saying "You look very nice today" is okay.

But is saying "Hey, great legs" always sexual harassment? It depends. It depends on the context—the who, what, where, when, why, and how—in which you say it. If you say it jokingly to a friend in shorts or a bathing suit and your friend laughs and says, "Yours aren't so bad either," then what you hear tells you that your statement wasn't perceived as harassment. If you say it to the new manager of human resources who has already told you to keep your remarks to yourself, then maybe it is.

Men who make gender-specific remarks to women as though women were objects, not individual people, are using sexual stereotypes to help them make sense of the world. And, no matter how complimentary the men may feel the remarks are, if these remarks are unwanted, they constitute sexual harassment. Because

some women might like being looked at and admired in some situations by some people doesn't mean that all women like it or that
women who like it sometimes will like it all the time. Talking that
way is asking for trouble; you must understand the particular context of your talk.

There's no substitute for sensitivity to each new situation and
each person we talk to. We can't behave toward the opposite sex
as though their gender identity tells us everything we need to know
about them. Each person must be recognized as the individual they
are, not as a symbol for their gender.

The better we know people, the harder it is to generalize about
them. The closer we are, the more complicated people become. It's
harder to describe a close friend than someone we know only casu-
ally. We all have our personal identity that overrides our gender
identity in practical, everyday, real-life situations.

Whether the generalizations made about women and men are
true doesn't necessarily matter. We're not dealing with women or
men in general. We're dealing with Margaret Smith or David
Brown. People are individuals with personal identities. We have
to talk to them based on what we know they're like, and we can
only know what they're like by getting to know them. If we treat
them as stereotypical women or men, we're ignoring the important
things about them.

Stereotypes turn us into objects. They take away our real being.
In doing business, no one wants to be treated as some stereotypical
customer; instead, people want to be talked to in ways that recognize their individuality. People who know how to do that know one
of the secrets of success.

Managing Uncertainty in Talk

In communicating with people from diverse backgrounds, we have
the same basic problems as communicating with anyone. We can
never know as much as we would like to about people's context for
understanding: their thinking, their motivations, their aspirations

and their other practical interests. This is the problem of uncertainty in communication.

We have to manage uncertainty in talk just as we manage all the other uncertainties in our daily lives. Every day we have to deal with many unanticipated problems. Will that order arrive on time? Am I going to have labor trouble if the contract negotiations don't work out? What's the marketplace going to be like six months from now? These problems arise through no fault of ours. They're a normal part of life. We live in a world in which our own lives are affected by the actions and decisions of people over whom we have little or no control.

When we have trouble communicating with people from different cultures, what we see are the normal problems of uncertainty compounded. We think we know even less about how they think than we do about people from our own culture. But the problem of communication doesn't change because of this. Regardless of the cultural identity of our colleagues, misunderstanding is normal. We understand each other by using all the contextual knowledge we have at our disposal. And this always includes many uncertainties.

Whether we're communicating with people from our own culture or different cultures, the opportunities for misunderstanding are endless. In some ways communication between people from the same culture has an even greater chance for misunderstanding because we assume we share an understanding and knowledge when often we do not. When we talk to people who look or sound different from us, at least we take less for granted. As a result, we may make context more explicit; in so doing, we increase the chances of understanding.

Clear communication with people from diverse backgrounds means taking less for granted. It means knowing that understanding happens when people share the same context for interpretation. When you can't be sure that the person you're talking to shares that context, then you must take steps to make it explicit by using formulations, asking questions, putting what others say into your own words, giving examples, and telling stories.

Treat Equals Equally and Unequals Unequally

We all have special formulas, proverbs, maxims, or rules of thumb that help us in our daily lives make the right decision or understand a situation better. In business "The customer is always right" is one of these, as is "The first one to market has the best chance of success." We've learned them from experience, or our favorite guru, or a current book. Our interpretation of them guides us through many aspects of our business lives.

One especially useful maxim is "Treat equals equally and treat unequals unequally," what R. S. Peters refers to as the principle of distributive justice. It means that we have to work at deciding whether people are the same or different in order to know how to treat them. It doesn't mean that one person or group is superior or inferior to another, only that sometimes we need to decide that people are the same, or different, for our practical purposes. It explains very well the kind of work we have to do to decide how to talk to people of different cultures or gender. We can't take it for granted that all blacks, women, men, Chicanos, or those from any other group have the same context for understanding talk. Each time we meet someone, we must work out how to talk to them by finding out their context for understanding. Discovering this also means creating the context in and through the talk itself.

Certainly there are real and relevant differences among cultures that come from cultural habits and values. The problem we face in interaction is knowing when those differences are relevant and when and how to use them. Knowing that real cultural differences exist between people doesn't tell us whether they are relevant in any situation of misunderstanding. We have to adapt for each interaction.

Consider the following incident described by Solomon in her *Wall Street Journal* article. It clearly illustrates the problem of cultural stereotyping, assuming that all people of the same cultural or ethnic identity interpret language using the same context for understanding.

A training film on cultural differences being shown at a Texas manufacturing plant shows a Native American woman working in an electronics plant. Her boss sees that she has found a better way to do the job. Ignoring her protests, he shouts to the other workers, "Hey, everybody, this is the kind of work I want to see!" The message of the film is that Native American culture emphasizes group harmony and cohesion so the boss was wrong to single the woman out. He caused her to lose face. In the next scene, the boss has changed. Now he is sensitive to Native American culture. He knows the error of his ways and simply offers the employee a letter for her personnel file.

But, Solomon reports, a Native American worker in that Texas plant got angry with this message. Her comment was, "I don't know what tribe that woman is from, maybe Navaho, but I'm Cherokee and I want public praise as much as the next person." Assuming that all Native Americans share the same attitudes toward public approbation has led to this misunderstanding. As Solomon says, "No matter how much we learn about cultures, we have to be aware of differences [within a culture] and of personal idiosyncracies and preferences." People's needs and reactions aren't the same across or within cultures. In fact, "the person who wants private recognition" may be "a blond California woman who just happens to be shy." As always, the solution is to ask—and listen to the answer. For example, the worker in the manufacturing plant told her boss not to draw attention to her. Unless he had good reason to believe that she was only being modest and really wouldn't object to it, he ought to have kept quiet. If he had any doubts about her sincerity, he should have said, "Are you sure you don't want me to say anything?"

Here's another example of the problem of deciding when cross-cultural differences are relevant as context. An Asian woman being interviewed for a job in the United States keeps her eyes down, not meeting those of the interviewer. Is she displaying her cultural background by deferring to authority, as her Asian culture demands? The manager conducting the interview might think the woman isn't assertive, not strong enough, hiding something, or insecure. Her behavior goes against everything the manager has been taught about interviewing. For her part, the Asian woman might interpret the interviewer's eye contact as domineering, invasive, and controlling.

If I place myself in the shoes of the interviewer, what's the practical value to me of labeling this woman's behavior as representative of her Asian culture? Let's assume that it's true that she avoids eye contact because in her original culture that was what women were expected to do. I can't change that, even if I wanted to. My concern is whether she can do the job that needs to be done in my organization. If this job needs someone who can interact easily with me and others, it doesn't matter to me what the woman's behavior represents. If I think the job requires eye contact, I won't hire her. But I should not conclude from this woman's behavior that all Asian women avoid eye contact or will behave in other ways as she does.

It may seem that we wear our cultural or gender identity like we wear clothing. But even if we're the same tribe or family, we're not all going to express ourselves the same way, think the same thoughts, or do the same things. We don't act out our cultural or gender identity like we act out a play on a stage. When we talk, we haven't memorized some cultural or gender script. If we had, we would sound like machines. Instead, we talk in ways that we think are appropriate to the situation in which we find ourselves. The reality is that we can't predict with any certainty what people will say simply from knowing that they're white or black, male or female Americans. We can't predict what anyone will say just from knowing their cultural identity or gender.

Recently I tried to solve an argument between two colleagues who were jointly authoring a book. They were bickering about the relative merits of their contributions. Their dispute threatened to end the project even though a publishing contract had been signed. As director of a research group that stood to profit financially, as well as academically, from the book, I had practical interests in trying to mediate as an interested and impartial third party. I got the two of them talking to me and eventually to each other. This discussion led to agreement on some issues. They also agreed to carry on in spite of their disagreements over other issues. It was the talking that did it. I had to talk to each of them on their own terms, but their cultural backgrounds never became a relevant issue in the negotiations. One was Canadian, the other South African. And I was American. Was there any relevant cultural knowledge that I needed about Canadians, South Africans, and Americans in order to solve the problem? I don't know. I can only say that it was never an issue.

I didn't say to myself, "I better learn about Canadian and South African culture so I know how to settle this dispute." Instead, I used my knowledge of the individuals involved, each of whom I had known for more than ten years. I also used my knowledge of how we misunderstand each other in talk. And I used my common sense (which may be different from yours). It worked—and the book has since been published.

Now think back to the example of the Native American woman. Do all of us have to learn about other cultures in order to communicate with them successfully? We have to be able to speak the same language (although sometimes even that's not necessary for clear communication). But must we all be experts in cross-cultural knowledge? Sometimes we may decide that cultural background makes a difference, and we need to use it in our interaction. But that decision comes out of the situation as we interpret it. It's not automatically there and not automatically a solution. Some people who know a great deal about cultural differences are poor communicators, even with people from their own cultures.

We all have to generalize about people. How we do so depends a lot on our own experiences and point of view. But we have to recognize what we lose when we do this. The more we generalize, the more we stand to risk creating and perpetuating misunderstanding.

Summary

Talk may be neither the cause nor the cure for all the problems of misunderstanding that stereotyping creates in organizations, but most stereotypes express themselves through language. Stereotyping means assuming that all members of an identifiable group share the same context for understanding. This may be the case, but it's not always so. Successful communication comes when we explicitly ensure shared context for understanding in each new interaction situation. Even when we all speak the same language, we may use or understand it differently as individuals.

Misunderstanding goes along with all language no matter who's talking and who's listening. Remember these points:

- Cultural and gender identities tell us what people *may* share but not what they *do* share.
- Differences within groups are normally greater than differences between groups.
- Shared context can't be taken for granted.
- A shared context for meaning can be established in and through talk.
- When understanding is critical, strategic talk is also.

In other words, in your everyday interaction with others, don't rely on stereotypical cultural and gender differences between people to tell you what to say or do. Try to forget about labels. Think about those to whom you talk as individuals. Think about what you know they're like as persons. Think about what they probably know or don't know. Think about what you have to do to get them to understand what you're saying; make the context of your thoughts explicit in the talk. Listen to what people are saying, and understand it for what it is. If you don't understand, don't try to be a mind reader. Tell people when you don't understand. Ask them questions. Put what you think they're saying in your own words, and ask them if that's what they meant.

Whatever you do, don't think you know someone simply because that's what "those people" say or that's a typical comment from that group. Even if you think that's true about that kind of person, make a real effort to overcome it. Thinking in stereotypes won't solve any communication problems and will only cause more. Concentrate instead on creating and discovering a shared context for understanding. That's more than enough work, but it will be worth it.

Checklist Part Two

Acknowledge that company policies, assignments, and rules always need interpretation.

Expect misunderstanding in communication between people inside and outside your organization because their contexts for understanding are different.

Don't assume that the parties to a negotiation understand each other until they show that they do explicitly in their talk.

Realize that as relationships and conditions change over time, we must sit down and talk face-to-face about what has happened and what is supposed to happen.

Don't rely on surveys, polls, or questionnaires to tell you what you need to know about the marketplace; you must work at sharing your consumer's context for meaning by using strategic talk.

Recognize that both spoken and written communication have problems of ambiguity and interpretation. The most effective written documents are interactive.

Acknowledge that the more critical the written communication, the more important that it be discussed by the person who wrote it and the people who have to understand and act on it.

Use concrete examples of what counts as doing the job in job descriptions and performance appraisal systems, combine the written job description and performance appraisal, and revise descriptions as part of each review.

Realize that although group and gender identity can be very important aspects of context, they are not automatically important. In fact, using gender and cultural stereotypes can contribute to misunderstanding by oversimplifying the issue of shared context. Much as generalizing makes it possible for us to communicate with each other about the world, it can also distort our world.

Never assume shared context—even within your own gender or group. Instead, talk to people as individuals rather than as members of groups.

Take less shared context for granted in communicating with people from diverse backgrounds. Decide whether people are the same or different in order to know how to treat them under the principle of distributive justice.

Part Three

What Your Organization Can Do to Help

Chapter Six

Building a Culture
That Supports Understanding

When we understand misunderstanding, we know that we have to get everyone to talk about what they don't understand. In theory and as a principle, that doesn't sound terribly difficult. But the reality demands work and practice. In a business setting, where people's jobs and livelihoods are at stake and where power and control figure in prominently, the mental shifts required for strategic talk can seem daunting.

Power and control are tools we can use to get work done within every organization. When they help us get work done effectively and efficiently, they make our jobs easier. But when they prevent us from talking to one another about critical issues because we're afraid to open our mouths, we have to rethink how they are used. This leaves us with a range of options. At one end is what happens now in most organizations: people use clarifying talk with great caution and only as a last resort in critical times, when they're sure they don't understand, when mistakes can't be tolerated, and when they trust the people they're talking to not to assume they're asking stupid questions. An unfortunate consequence is that many instances that are truly critical slip through without benefit of strategic talk. The other end of the range is seen in organizational cultures in which everyone is expected to clarify whatever they don't clearly understand. In such organizations, the responsibility to use strategic talk is on the speaker and the listener.

Often the problem of misunderstanding is bigger than the individual and intimately tied to the organization's style of doing and understanding things, of using power and control. In these cases, we have to find new ways to create a culture of clear communication that can support individual efforts at devising shared context and interpretation.

Using Power to Ensure Talk for Understanding

Once people within an organization understand that they have the freedom to talk about what they don't understand, they can then use talk to clarify the very information that the lack of talk hides. Across most organizations, there are topics and areas of concern that people feel they could never talk about with their boss. They're afraid to show they don't understand or that they're not clear about something because they expect negative consequences for not knowing. Thinking that words are normally clear and unambiguous, they're afraid that they're to blame for not clearly understanding. This fear gets in the way of people making sense of each other. To overcome the written and unwritten rules that keep people quiet, we need a commitment from those who have the power to open up the organization to free and easy communication.

Consider the example of Fedmet Inc., a distributor and processor of steel products with more than fifty-six locations in the United States and Canada. As Bruce Little reported on September 1, 1992, the company encourages people to speak their minds at "no-holds-barred" meetings. Management listens more than talks. The president delights in "the chaos that pervades his firm," believing that it encourages worker self-motivation and self-direction.

The new practice of talking in this way translates into teams of workers and managers ignoring titles and sharing information. The organizational design has a structure, but its flexibility allows new ways of doing and learning. Joint solution of problems comes from teams of people working and talking to each other.

How did these changes come about? Wayne Mang, the president, got the idea while flying to a meeting at which he was to describe the state of the company to local managers and workers. At the meeting, instead of doing all the talking himself, he got others to tell their views of the company's present state and needs. This led to a series of town meetings involving everyone who worked for the company, where anyone could say whatever they wished with no fear of reprisal.

Meetings like this sometimes damage the status quo, he said, and "it often takes several weeks to put it back together again." His statement underscores some of the benefits of the approach he used. It forces people to take risks and then grow from the consequences. It creates stress, stress from which the people of the organization learn and prosper.

In fact, productivity and employee morale within the company improved markedly as a result of these meetings and the changes they occasioned. Workers reduced setup time, improved customer response rates, and increased maintenance to reduce downtime. Production increased 50 percent in one month. On-time delivery, which was 58 percent in 1991, rose to 90 percent in 1992 and topped 94 percent by June 1993. The first quarter of 1993 showed a rise in sales of 9 percent in the United States and almost 5 percent in Canada. First-quarter profits for 1993 were higher than for all of 1992. Given the state of the economy, these figures, reported by Little in a follow-up article on June 16, 1993, are singularly impressive.

A few points are worth emphasizing so that we can learn from Fedmet's experience. This company used the power of talk to flatten the organizational hierarchy so that everyone could express their views and share information for the benefit of the company as a whole. Their new way of working gave them the freedom to talk to one another in new ways. Their new way of talking to one another benefited everyone.

Every organization must become open to the power of talk, even though the changes entailed might seem disruptive in the short term. In the long term there is no better way to ensure understanding.

Understanding the Need for Clear Communication

For clarity, whether in performing tasks as routine as noting telephone messages or in transmitting a corporate vision, we all must expect misunderstanding and know how to prevent it. The manager of a video satellite receiver company was faced with the reality of these needs recently. She'd been trying for months, without much success, to get her salespeople to realize that vastly improved customer service was the most important part of their current push to regain market share. Customer complaints about poor, inefficient, and costly service showed that the company had serious communication problems, which was ironic since they were in the communications business. Her problem was how to get the managers to see and understand her vision of immediate, efficient, and effective response to all service needs. In frustration she put the following question to me: "What do I have to do to make myself perfectly clear?" My answer came from what I have learned about shared understanding: "I think you have to use talk to create a context for the salespeople to use to interpret your vision. You've got to have a conversation about the company with everyone involved: where it's been, where it is, and where it's going. You can agree, disagree, whisper, shout, argue 'til the cows come home. Carry on until everyone understands each other's views. Then build on this shared understanding to shape your vision. If this vision is critical to your company's health, don't stop talking until you're all too weak to carry on."

This is a bit of an exaggeration. But in essence it shows what must be done. There are no shortcuts. We have to use normal everyday language systematically to help others understand our vision. There's no better way to prevent misunderstanding than by using ordinary talk to say what's on our minds, asking simple and not so simple questions, checking to see if we're being clear, making our context explicit, and getting everyone in the company to do the same thing with each other and with their customers and suppliers. Talk won't eliminate all misunderstanding, but it will do a better job than other techniques available to us. It works because through it we can hear each other's understanding out loud. If we want to provide leadership and direction, we don't want to depend on people reading our minds.

For talk effectively to improve an organization, we have to make open lines of communication a top priority. The hazards of closed, hierarchical communication networks are revealed in the following story, the essence of which occurs in organization after organization. Edwin, a longtime employee of a major airline, was brilliant at his job in ground maintenance and was promoted to a management position. From his experience as shop foreman he brought with him many excellent ideas for making local and national maintenance operations more cost-effective. Although he discussed these ideas with his immediate superior, he got no response from the head office. He found it increasingly difficult to sit back and watch the waste and inefficiency in the operation, but he felt powerless to change it. He wasn't interested in promotion but in the well-being of the company. After two years in the management job, having had little opportunity to speak to anyone in senior management about his ideas, the feelings of frustration and powerlessness led Edwin to seek other employment. It was only at his exit interview that the company seemed at all interested in what he had to say. They were surprised to hear his complaints about the difficulty he had in communicating his ideas and said they thought the company had developed open lines of communication.

Many large organizations have difficulty giving a high priority to looking into our hearts and minds and understanding our goals, thoughts, and feelings as they affect the company. We have to spell them out if they're important. But the organizational policies and structures must be in place to let us do it. Successful organizations will work at creating a culture for communication that opens up opportunities for face-to-face talk between and among all levels.

On the other hand, there are limits. In our normal, everyday talk, we don't always need to understand everyone and every statement precisely. We needn't press everyone to make themselves crystal clear in each interaction; if we did, they might think we were crazy. People don't expect or need precision in most conversations, even within the organization.

Imagine that the chairperson of an organization to which you belong has faxed you a list of names and telephone numbers and asked that you remind people of the monthly luncheon. If you intend to delegate this task to someone, what will you say, how much detail will you provide? Your explanation might be simple: "I'm a university representative on a research and development association, and I've been asked to remind the people on this list about a luncheon next Tuesday. Would you mind making the calls for me? Just call on my behalf and remind the people that there's a luncheon next week." Assuming the person agrees, you could provide information on the details of the luncheon and the names and phone numbers of the people to call. You wouldn't expect to field questions about the request. Details such as precisely when to call, in what order to call, what to say, whether or not it is necessary to speak directly to the person named, and whether speaking to a machine or leaving a message with someone else is acceptable wouldn't seem to warrant discussion. You could assume, with reasonable safety, that the person would know what to do and how to do it. And in the great scheme of things, if someone, or even everyone, on the list didn't get the message in time, got the wrong message, or didn't get the message at all, it wouldn't be a catastrophe. It would be unfortunate, annoying, and poor practice. But as a one-time occurrence, understanding this request couldn't be considered critical to the organization.

However, suppose that you're arranging a meeting with your associates and the principals of a company you're hoping to buy. The time lines are very tight and the sellers aren't highly motivated to sell. In such a circumstance, you'd be very careful in relating the exact message to be given to your associates and that each must receive the message directly; the message should not be left on a machine or given to another person. You'd also want the calls to begin right away and be completed well in advance of the meeting. Under these circumstances, your request must be phrased with utmost precision so that it is accurately carried out and the proposed buyout isn't threatened.

Part of building a culture of understanding through talk means teaching everyone to use the techniques of strategic talk selectively. It means focusing efforts and energies to help ensure that others hear and understand our goals, aspirations, dreams, purposes, and motivations the way we intend. There's no better way to achieve this common interpretation than through talk. We can help create an atmosphere of trust by talking and listening to people in our organization in the same way we would talk or listen to friends. First, and always, we must demonstrate a selfless interest in what others have to say—and without overtly judging them. People will talk when they think they have nothing to fear from saying what's on their minds. But beyond our actions as individuals, what can be done to encourage clear communication?

Policies and structures can be established to help ensure that the power of everyday talk is realized appropriately. Policies that reinforce open and clear communication and structures that support it are critical. And operational reliability depends on them.

Policies and Structures to Ensure Clear Communication

Even the best manager can't manage everything all the time: to a large extent, organizations must operate themselves. The process must run smoothly most of the time, or a company will go out of business. Everyone must know how to do their jobs well and without constant supervision.

If our organizations are to run smoothly without constant management, we must recognize that we can't take clear communication for granted. We must recognize that everyone perceives the world in a different way. We can't assume that people who are members of the organization automatically understand that world in the same way. Objects, ideas, and events don't have the same meaning for everyone, not even for those we know well or with whom we've worked over a period of time. We must expect misunderstanding and help prevent it by creating an organization in which two-way communication is demanded. One component in that approach is to establish and support policies that make for easy communication within and between all levels.

Policies

There are steps we can take to establish organizational goals and to structure personnel and operations for clear communication. These steps are a beginning; changing and building an organizational culture that has clear communication at the core of its policies and structures is an ongoing task. In the following sections, we describe some of the policies, from opening lines of communication to developing communication skills, that can be implemented to aid in clear communication.

Open lines of communication. Shared interpretation can't be taken for granted; we have to work at making it happen. Yet few organizations have policies that actively encourage clear communication within the organization and with its clients and customers.

Misunderstanding frequently happens between organizations and their clients because there's no communication policy in place that makes it easy for customers to talk about product or service problems. But there are easy ways to prevent this kind of misunderstanding. For instance, the companies that make customer service a priority often require their salespeople to make regular follow-up calls to customers. In this way, they can ensure that no problems with their product will happen as a result of misunderstandings. This additional contact helps the companies avoid surprise customer complaints and problems. Talk between the salespeople and the customers links the companies with the marketplace and is an important element in a strategy that competes in the market through providing outstanding customer service.

Remember that people always provide their own interpretation of language. Therefore, in order for everyone to understand each other—whether on the issue of market share, what to do about it, and whose responsibility it is or on the importance of returning phone calls—there must be talk about it. When the situation is critical, a speech, no matter how powerful or convincing, won't do. Instead, people need conversation. Conversations can be used for every task from explaining current sales to encouraging people to work harder and be more competitive; at the same time, they serve as a check on the other side of the story. In conversations, we can learn how people understand our position and their own.

Naturally, you can't possibly talk to everyone. But you can talk to your people, who can then talk to their people, who talk to their people. It's amazing how many people you can talk to if you have the right motivation. If you need motivation, consider a report by Albert Karr of a survey of CEOs of 164 large companies. The survey showed that most of the CEOs said that "personal communication helps workers' job satisfaction and commitment" and results in improved earnings. Most of the CEOs questioned also said that because of other demands, they couldn't afford to give more time to communicating with their people. Yet in critical situations, they can't afford not to.

Alan Farnham of *Fortune* magazine reported on some additional studies. A survey done by Forum Corporation found that 82 percent of Fortune 500 executives believed that their corporate strategy is understood by "everyone who needs to know." But is this perception accurate? A Louis Harris study indicating that "less than a third of employees say management provides clear goals and direction" points to a large gap between perception and reality. As Karr has reported, this is further buttressed by Professor Robert Kelley of Carnegie Mellon University, who found that nearly 70 percent of the 400 corporate executives he asked believed that business leaders fail to get their goals across to employees.

Discrepancies and disagreements like those just cited are themselves indications of the problems of understanding each other. Poll and survey questions are as indexical as any other language. Therefore, they can only be a first step to probing more deeply into what people actually mean when they answer a survey questionnaire. Remember, if you really want to know people's thoughts or opinions, you have to talk to them at some length to find out exactly what they mean.

If corporate strategy and goals are important, then organizations must take extraordinary steps to communicate them clearly. The solution to the problem of clear communication isn't mysterious. Nor can we find it in polls or questionnaires. The solution rests in talk.

Support questions. Silence isn't golden when clear communication is crucial. Every organization should have a policy that encourages and rewards people for taking the time to talk about work and work-related issues. The policy has to convince and demonstrate to employees that questions, even those that might sound obvious, should be asked. Without constant clarification, misunderstanding will surface only when things go wrong. Clear communication depends on constant feedback at every level. The sooner misunderstanding is recognized, the sooner it can be corrected. Keep the adage "Bad news never improves with age" firmly in mind.

The responsibility to recognize, fix, and communicate about problems must be within the appropriate person's operational area. There's no substitute for experiential understanding; no one can understand any operation completely without actually having done it. Shared experience of doing a job is the best context for understanding any communication about it.

If managers and supervisors are to understand front-line problems, successes, and ideas for change, they must talk to employees on a regular basis. It isn't possible to know about the work if they talk only as a part of performance appraisals.

Build a culture of clear communication based on an atmosphere of trust and understanding. You must be trusted if you hope to make clear communication the number one priority in your organizations. If people think that their talk isn't valued or will be used against them, they'll stop talking. Only in an atmosphere of trust where everyone understands why misunderstanding happens will people feel free to ask questions or say they don't understand. Such a culture is best built by example from the top down. Some suggestions on how to do it through talk follow:

- Ask real questions. Real questions are those whose answer you don't already know. You may think that you never ask questions if you already know the answer. But you do. For instance, in talking with an associate, you might ask, "Have you returned Jeanne's phone call yet?" The response "No, not yet" prompts you to say, "Yes, I know. I just spoke to Jeanne on another matter and she said you still haven't called." In this case, you already knew the answer and were testing the other person. If people hear you asking such questions too often while pretending they are real questions, they'll stop trusting you. They'll begin to think your questions are tests rather than ways to gather information.

- Consider others' talk as a window on the "nuts and bolts" world of your operation. Don't use what you know to make that talk seem out of place or unimportant. You may have a different context for understanding the big picture, you may have more information available to you, but you can't understand the big picture if you sacrifice the small picture. If people think you don't value their talk, they may stop talking.

- Verbally reward people for talking about the organization with you. Tell them that you value their comments. Ask them questions to help you understand better what they're saying. You might say, "That's something I've never thought about," "Why do you think that's the case?" or "Who do you think might best deal with this problem?" Show others their talk is valued by making the appropriate response that indicates you heard and understood what they were saying. If you didn't, then say so and talk with them until you do.

Supplement written communication on critical issues with talk. No matter how careful or skilled you are as a writer or how apparently clear your writing, never assume that readers will give the written word the interpretation you intended. This extends throughout the organization. In fact, it should be an organization's policy that writers of all critical memos, reports, letters, and contracts must talk about those documents with the people who need to know.

Some companies try to communicate their visions and policies through written material. Written memos, directives, and newsletters are good but not good enough. The ambiguity of language makes memos on critical issues a hazardous method of communication. We have little control over our readers' interpretations unless we can talk to them. Therefore, when any critical changes in organizational direction are afoot, managers and employees should meet and talk. That's the only way to ensure that everyone understood the changes in the way intended.

Create or support a specialized language for communication of critical information. People working in critical areas can be trained to use a language with special words and meanings that are more precise than normal language. This policy has its benefits—and its problems. On the plus side, people versed in the specialized language can carry on talk that is less ambiguous than it would be using normal, everyday language. On the minus side, people who haven't been trained in the language will be less likely to understand what's going on, and there may be situations in which this lack of understanding can do serious harm. Nevertheless, specialized language is used in many occupations and professions to make it easier to communicate clearly to those involved on a regular basis.

The overall communication structure of an organization is only as strong as the communication skills of each person in the organization. Every organization should have it as a matter of policy that all employees must understand how to anticipate misunderstanding and take the appropriate steps to fix it. Developing people's communication skills through human resource development can help this happen. John Raymond gave a specific instance of this in a recent column. As he reported, when John Morgan was acting as president of Labatt Breweries, he said:

> One of the key responsibilities of any CEO is a total commitment to education and training. If we can educate the human resource at our disposal, then we can tap that resource—all the time. People want to participate and use their initiative. When they participate, results go up and they're willing to

put forward the hard options. Harnessing that spells success. People have the answers. The problem is that nobody asks them the questions.

Everyone should be trained in communication skills. Those who need a specialized language should be thoroughly trained in it. Specific steps and structures for this are covered in the discussion of structures.

Structures

Policies that open up the organization to strategic talk are useful. However, it also helps to put positive structures in place that enhance the opportunities to create shared context and shared understanding. As we begin to use strategic talk, we can create structures in which even more strategic talk is possible. Some of these structures must be created by management and instituted throughout the organization; others can be started less formally. Through them, everyone can work toward the goal of clear understanding.

Continual training. All employees should participate in regular training programs. Training creates a common context for understanding what they and their co-workers are doing and talking about in all aspects of doing the job.

At Pacific Gas and Electric Corporation (PG&E) in California, operational reliability ranks as a number one priority. Clear communication forms an essential part of this reliability. The workers in PG&E's generating stations train for one week out of every four. Workers learn about their own jobs and those of others. This shared context makes misunderstanding much less likely. As Lascher and La Porte have documented, PG&E's efforts have paid off: their electrical services have been available on the average 99.965 percent of the time they were requested.

Mediated communication. Not every person in the organization will be able to understand, operate, or make decisions in areas in which they don't normally work. The organization should therefore be structured so that someone who is familiar with both sides of an operation can act as an intermediary when people have to communicate across operational boundaries. For example, managers can be prepared to act as communication links across operations; as a step in this, the managers must be trained to see and know the big picture. Use of cross-training and joint meetings will enhance this ability. Cross-training in business copies cross-training in physical conditioning. A distance runner will also swim, cycle, and lift weights to improve physical and mental conditioning beyond what simply running might do. Managers in production can spend six days each year (one day every second month) working in marketing, sales, customer relations, distribution, legal, whatever areas are appropriate. Such cross-training can be increased between interdependent areas that might be experiencing communication problems.

Backups. Overlapping responsibility creates an important structural safeguard for clear communication. In critical operational areas, more than one person must be available who understands the job and who can communicate it to others. This backup protects the communication process in the organization when illness, some emergency situation, or other instance prevents the person normally responsible from doing his or her job.

Inverted pyramid for clear communication. People can solve problems if they can talk about them. Everyone in an organization should be trained to ask questions in situations of misunderstanding, top down and bottom up. Managers can manage effectively when they can talk to their bosses about organizational problems. We can all can be more effective if we're free to ask questions. We can't solve problems if we can't talk about them. For these reasons, it is important to open the lines of two-way communication, keep them open, and ensure that communication can happen from the bottom up. In fact, organizations that value clear communication depend on bottom-up communication. Yet very few organizations have the kind of free and open atmosphere in which it is easy to ask questions from the bottom up. Since many people still believe that the need for questions indicates incompetence, that should come as no surprise.

Amanda, president of an advertising agency, and her assistant, Jessica, have been working together for two and a half years. You might expect them to be so familiar with each other's work habits and ways of expressing themselves that they could almost communicate without talking. Sometimes they can. But not always. For example, this exchange took place early one afternoon.

Amanda: Is that report ready?

Jessica: No, not yet. I've been working on that contract you gave me this morning.

Amanda: That could have waited. We need that report for this afternoon.

Jessica: But you told me to get that contract done and out of here right away. I know how important it is.

Amanda: But you should have realized we need that report for the meeting this afternoon.

Jessica: When you gave me that contract this morning you said, "Get this done and out right away." Naturally I thought you meant it.

Amanda: I know that's what I said, but you should have known what I meant.

Jessica heard Amanda's instructions. She thought she knew what Amanda meant: stop working on the report and get the contract done, then finish the report needed for that day. Unfortunately, Amanda thought Jessica would understand that the report should be given first priority. If Amanda had made clear communication top priority, Jessica would have been more inclined to question Amanda concerning which project Jessica was to complete first.

Misunderstanding someone else's sense of priorities is common. We all know from our experience that our words don't always communicate what we want them to. "Do this and get it out right away" sounds simple and clear. But if we don't get the intended results, we have to recognize that it was neither simple nor clear.

Policies and structures cover the measurable, business side of talk. Yet another side of talk is always at work. All of our conversations, regardless of the topic, are grounded in social and personal interests as well. To be effective, our talk must recognize this and accommodate for it.

Recognizing the Personal Within the Culture

People need to talk to each other in organizations, and about more than business. They need to talk in order to maintain their relationships. An executive open-door policy helps support this. Its rewards come from the talk itself and not from what the talk is about. Talking to people, regardless of the content, goes a long way toward producing a desirable corporate culture.

Maintaining Social Relationships

One of the principal functions of talk has nothing to do with exchanging information and everything to do with maintaining relationships. Research into how we talk shows that we use it to avoid or minimize conflict and maintain friendly relationships with people. Good social relationships in organizations make it possible for us to enjoy talking to the people with whom we live and work for many hours each day, week after week, year after year. Maintaining these relationships means knowing how to avoid offending or embarrassing others unintentionally. This, too, is an important part of creating a culture for understanding.

To maintain these good relationships, we have to know how to respond to unwanted invitations, offers, and requests in ways that save face for everyone involved. As an example, consider what happened as Amy approached Jack, her associate in the company, in the hall outside his office:

> *Amy:* Jack, how about having lunch with me today so we can discuss that new marketing strategy you mentioned the other day?

Jack: No.

Amy looked at Jack for a moment, then turned and walked away.

Does this encounter strike you as odd? No doubt you read Jack's reply to Amy's invitation as abrupt, rude, and antisocial, and you expect that Amy felt the same way about it. This interchange could threaten Amy and Jack's social and professional relationship. Instead, a more gracious response could have been "Amy, thanks for the invitation. Unfortunately, I already have a commitment for lunch that I can't break. How about tomorrow?" Jack's excuse doesn't have to be strictly true. In fact, he may simply want to do something else. But his new response to Amy's invitation sounds much better because it gives Amy a good reason why Jack can't accept. It avoids conflict or loss of face. And in suggesting an alternative time, Jack shows that he has no objection to having a business meal with Amy. This answer maintains the existing relationship between Amy and Jack.

Bear in mind that the length of the conversation isn't critical. For instance, under different circumstances, Amy and Jack's initial conversation could have gone like this:

Amy: Jack, how about having lunch with me today so we can discuss that new marketing strategy you mentioned the other day?

Jack: Sure.

Amy: I'll meet you at Côte Basque at one.

Jack: Fine.

In this exchange, Jack's responses were brief and monosyllabic, as in the first one. The important difference is that this time he gave the answer that promoted social solidarity; he gave what's called the preferred response. This response met Amy's business need to discuss the marketing strategy and her personal need to feel comfortable with her co-worker. The latter is just one personal need; many others also must be attended to in building a culture of understanding.

Understanding Others' Practical Interests

We all have personal practical interests—motives, expectations, desires, ambitions, and fears—that create part of the context for understanding other's talk. Successful communication, and successful leadership, means understanding that those practical interests will affect the way others understand what we're saying. We also have to realize that these interests will affect the meaning of what others say. Unfortunately, others don't always share our interests, and often we don't recognize theirs.

Have you ever said something to a business associate that you thought was going to help that person do a better job, advance the person's career, and generally improve the organization, only to have it thrown accusingly back in your face? Your interest was to show concern. You thought your comment clearly expressed that. Instead, what the person heard was criticism, either personal or of the work at hand.

Take, for example, the following situation. The senior manager of a large, midwestern real estate company could see that a new person in her office who had been given the receptionist job temporarily was struggling with the job. The person looked a mess and seemed very tired and drawn. So the manager called the new employee into her office:

Shelly: How're you doing?

John: I'm really tired.

Shelly: You look tired. Would you like to take a couple of weeks off? I could get someone to fill in for you until you feel better.

John: No.

Shelly: Are you sure? You really look like you need a rest from this job.

John: I can't believe you're saying this to me! You just told me to leave because I don't look good.

Shelly: That's not what I meant.

John: But that's what you said.

Shelly: Not at all.

John left Shelly's office and, much to Shelly's dismay, proceeded to clear out his desk and leave. Shelly thinks it is unlikely John will be back. According to Shelly, John completely misinterpreted her meaning. She'd approached their conversation with concern for John's health and ability to do the job; she thought a short break might help. As manager, Shelly wanted the person at the reception desk to convey a bright, welcoming image to people coming into the office. She was concerned on a personal and professional level when John appeared ill dressed and looking unfit. She believed that the best way to resolve the problem was to speak directly to John about her concerns. She thought she was making herself perfectly clear—and doing everything that interpersonal communications consultants would approve.

Unfortunately, what John heard wasn't Shelly's concern for his personal well-being but simply that he was being asked to leave his job because he didn't look good. John heard Shelly's comments in light of his own interests, which were probably related to keeping his job. The meaning, or intention, or motive, of Shelly's comments thus became a matter of how John interpreted her comments. This is shown in John's reply, which is at odds with what Shelly had in mind. All communication in interaction works this way. The person we're talking to interprets our talk and creates its meaning in each instance. The interpretation we intend may not be heard; unless the people to whom we talk make their understanding of our statements explicit, we can't know how they interpreted our words. Multiple interpretations can be made of almost any statement.

We must recognize that people's practical interests will often get in the way of understanding. Knowing this is a step toward understanding. We can make our own interests explicit through using the conversational techniques we've already learned: be explicit, check for understanding using questions, paraphrase, use examples, and tell stories. We can also formulate what we imagine or consider others' practical interests to be.

For example, once their conversation opened, Shelley could have said, "John, you're an excellent salesperson. I'm not criticizing your work and I don't want you to take this the wrong way. But you don't look well. I'm concerned about your health and the fact that the receptionist work doesn't seem to suit you. I think you could benefit from a few weeks off. What do you think?" Putting it this way makes Shelley's views explicit and also gives John a chance to agree or disagree. Whatever he says will provide the context for subsequent talk in that conversation. In this way both Shelley's and John's practical concerns are made explicit.

Once again it is clear that we must make our interpretation of meaning explicit. And we have to get others to do the same. If we don't, we've no way of knowing how they understood what we were saying. Shared understanding means that talk flows in both directions.

Using Talk to Ensure Understanding

Just as Shelley was upset that her conversation with John took a turn she hadn't intended, the CEOs of many organizations seem to be regularly upset because their intentions, policies, or actions are misinterpreted. This misunderstanding is especially a problem at times of crisis management. If our company oil tanker has just run aground and created an international pollution disaster, we want to be sure that people understand our side of the story.

As a less catastrophic example, consider the insurance industry. Insurance companies are poorly understood by their clients and the general public because their business is associated with personal and public tragedy and because of the supposed level and source of their profits. The industry wants to improve communication with their clients and the general public through an effective public relations campaign as the most immediate solution to the problem. But any public relations campaign must still grapple with the questions we face whenever we try to make people understand:

Who talks?

What do we talk about?

Where do we talk?

When do we talk?

Why do we talk?

How do we talk so that people interpret us as we intend them to?

The particulars of who, when, and even where can't be determined without knowledge of the why—why the insurance industry wants points communicated—and what points those are. Much of this information must come from public relations people experienced with the matters at hand. But, if understanding is to occur, the task requires talk, dialogue, and give-and-take. Regardless of the ethical questions of truth and accuracy of facts, if you want to be understood, you must use strategic talk. We may think we're expressing ourselves very clearly and directly. But everyone listening will be making their own interpretations, which may or may not be what we intended. If we want people to understand clearly, then what we say can't be separated from how we say it.

Summary

To build a culture of understanding, we must know that in practice, words don't have just one meaning. We must therefore determine how to communicate the right meaning to people in our organizations.

We can help eradicate misinterpretation by changing our culture and our daily practices. To begin we must work at making our understanding clear through talk. If we don't, we will be continually frustrated by misunderstanding, which will exact a heavy price in terms of organizational efficiency and morale. This isn't simply people choosing not to communicate with others; it is our normal, everyday communication practices in which people want to be understood. Once we're committed to clear communication through talk, we can focus on creating a shared context for inter-pretation with others throughout the organization.

People must come to know that it is safe to say, "I don't under-stand. Can you clarify that for me?" People must be able to ask questions with confidence and without fear. We must all under-stand the fundamentals of how talk works in practice so we won't feel uncomfortable in asking questions, whether of management, employees, or suppliers.

Creating such a culture doesn't happen overnight. It takes weeks, months, and sometimes years of practicing what we preach. The commitment must be more than just talk. We must not only say we value talk to ensure understanding; we must also show that we value talk by creating and supporting policies and structures to reinforce this commitment. Policies and structures as described in this chapter and augmented in practice can create the proper con-text for the kind of talk that leads to understanding.

Chapter Seven

Communicating When Understanding Is Critical

If misunderstanding rarely happened, the fact that people generally expect us to understand what they say the first time wouldn't cause problems. However, if people within an organization misunderstand each other on a regular basis, their misunderstanding can do critical damage to the organization. A terrible waste of resources, both human and financial, is bound to occur. Examining the priorities and methods of organizations known as high-reliability organizations (HROs) can help us identify our own priorities for clear communication and show us how to support them.

In effect, every organization needs to be a HRO in most of its operations. However, HROs have one main objective: to maintain the highest levels of operational reliability. They can't afford misunderstanding because the consequences of the operational mistakes that might result can mean that people die, space shuttles explode, planes crash, nuclear reactors melt down, deadly chemicals spew forth, and cities and towns lose essential services. People in HROs work hard to create shared context, provide systems that check understanding, give people responsibility for ensuring that their messages or actions are clearly received and understood, create backup communication systems, and make more than one person responsible for communicating the same information.

Yet in spite of their systems and methods, HROs experience misunderstanding. The occasional failure of 911 emergency response systems and air traffic control systems and the *Challenger* space shuttle disaster show evidence of serious misunderstanding. That doesn't mean that their systems are worthless. Quite the opposite. They're a step in the right direction because they recognize the ubiquity of misunderstanding and have developed elaborate systems in their organizations to try to compensate. But they're not foolproof; they're not enough in themselves.

Consequences of Misunderstanding

All organizations have some problems with misunderstanding. The consequences of misunderstanding can range from little more than having to rephrase a question to human deaths. Although for most of us, misunderstanding is not normally a matter of life and death, in 911 emergency response organizations, it's often exactly that.

Emergency-response units organized to respond to 911 calls and other organizations that operate "on the edge" place operational reliability at the top of their priorities. Yet misunderstandings still happen despite the fact that the people who answer, evaluate, and act on 911 calls are trained to talk to people who are under great emotional and physical stress and to get the best possible result for the people involved in the emergency. Callers to 911 are often incoherent, distressed, and in no fit state to have a telephone conversation. As Tupper Hull reported in the *Dallas Times Herald* in 1984:

> Dallas Fire Department officials are investigating an incident in which an ambulance was delayed seven minutes while a dispatcher argued with a man who said his stepmother was dying in his home. When paramedics were sent to the East Dallas home 13 minutes later, they found the woman dead. A claim, filed with the city by [the caller], seeks $300,000 in damages from the city in connection with the Jan. 5 death of his stepmother.

The record of the call reveals that first the caller and the desk operator, and then the caller and the nurse, weren't making sense of each other's talk. The cause of the misunderstanding seems to be that each person had a different context for understanding what should be said next. The caller knew that his stepmother needed medical attention as soon as possible and wanted an ambulance sent; the fire department operator knew that she must direct the call to the appropriate service and wanted as much information as possible to do this properly; the nurse knew that she needed the full details of the medical emergency so she could provide appropriate help.

In the following transcript of the call (included as part of an article by Whalen, Zimmerman, and Whalen), D refers to the fire department desk operator who initially received the call; C, to the caller; and N, to the nurse-dispatcher.

D: Fire department.

C: Yes, I'd like to have an ambulance at forty-one thirty-nine Haverford please.

D: What's the problem, sir?

C: I don't know, and if I knew I wouldn't be calling you all.

D: Are you the one that needs the ambulance?

C: No, I am not. It's my mother.

D: Let me let you speak with the nurse.

C: Oh, bullshit!

N: This is the fire department nurse, what is the address?

C: Forty-one thirty-nine Haverford.

N: Forty-one thirty-nine, what's the street?

C: [Drive]

C: Haverford Drive (in irritated tone of voice).

N: H-A-V-E-O-R-D.

C: No. H-A-V-E-R-F-O-R-D. Drive.

N: Okay. Is this a house or an apartment?

C: It's a home.

N: What street crosses Haverford there on the corner?

C: Uh, it's Lincoln, you can cut off at Lincoln . . .

N: And the phone number?

C: The phone number, three two nine, three two two five.

N: And what is the problem there?

C: I don't know, if I knew I wouldn't be needing you.

N: Sir, would you answer my questions please? What is the problem?

C: She's having difficulty in breathing.

N: How old is this person?

C: She's sixty years old.

N: Where is she now?

C: She's in the bedroom right now.

N: May I speak with her, please?

C: No, you can't. She seems like she's incoherent.

N: Why is she incoherent?

C: How the hell do I know!

From this point on matters get even worse. Eventually C hangs up. His roommate calls back, and the nurse informs him that the ambulance has been dispatched. But by the time the paramedics arrived, the stepmother was dead.

We can think of a call to 911 as a type of service call. We make service calls to get the air conditioning fixed, the dishwasher repaired, the carpets cleaned, or to order lunch. Calling our local pizza place to order a twelve-inch pie with mushrooms and pepperoni but no anchovies is a service call. We would expect the pizza person just to take our name and address and send our order out as soon as possible, not to ask, "Why do you need a pizza?" The caller to 911 might have been in the pizza call context. That would explain why he said what he did. The questions from the desk operator and the nurse would have seemed strange and unnecessary; from his perspective, the 911 operator should have just taken his order and sent an ambulance as soon as possible. Instead, the operator and the nurse weren't in the pizza call context. They were in the 911 context; they needed details and reasons so they could make the appropriate response.

But the caller wasn't giving the right answers to their questions. We don't know why and we can't. We can't read his mind. We might just as well ask why, when the nurse heard the caller say that his stepmother was having difficulty breathing, the nurse didn't immediately send out the paramedics. Trying to read others' minds may be interesting, but it gets us no closer to knowing what was actually going on inside their heads. All we can know is what they actually said and did. And in this case, that added up to a serious misunderstanding because contexts were so different.

Misunderstandings such as this aren't uncommon. In giving a presentation to a group of businesspeople in a management communication course, I used this 911 episode as an example of misunderstanding. I pointed out that calling 911 is probably a rare experience for most of us and asked how many of the group had ever had to call 911. A woman raised her hand. I asked her to tell her story.

She had called 911 because her husband had suddenly become quite ill. She gave them her address, but the address was misunderstood and the paramedics went to the wrong place. She could hardly hold back the tears as she told us that by the time the paramedics finally arrived, her husband was dead. Nothing could have brought home more forcefully the need to know how to ensure clear communication in crucial situations.

In Chapter Four, I describe another tragic example of misunderstanding in the events leading up to the *Challenger* space shuttle disaster. Miscommunication occurred between engineers and management, with each interpreting data from different perspectives. Researcher Dorothy Winsor clearly found that "communication isn't just shared information; it's shared interpretation."

The *Challenger* exploded because of the failure of a rubber O-ring seal and its backup seal in the booster rocket. For the personnel of Morton Thiokol International (MTI), the Marshall Space Center, and NASA, miscommunication centered on the difficulty of sharing the same understanding of the O-ring problem and knowing whether the potential failure of the O-rings to seal the field joints was serious enough to postpone the launch of the shuttle.

From written memos and testimony it's difficult to know who really said what to whom. However, clearly different people gave different interpretations to the problem and its seriousness.

In this disaster, the many levels of organization in the space program worked against clear communication because they didn't provide the opportunity for the people making the final decisions to talk problems through with the people most closely involved with the problems. The organizational structure made it difficult for people to share interpretations because it separated the communication from the communicator. It separated the words from their context.

We can't assume that the fact that the engineers and management were from different corporate subcultures caused the miscommunication. Even sharing corporate roles and, by implication, corporate concerns and values doesn't ensure shared interpretation. If time and proximity don't assure understanding, what can improve the chances for it?

Systems to Help Prevent Misunderstanding

In order to prevent misunderstanding, HROs have tried to devise systems to ensure clear communication. We can learn some useful lessons from their successes and failures and combine them with what we already know about misunderstanding.

The structures and policies of HROs recognize that misunderstanding is likely unless we take special steps to prevent it, including those listed here:

- *Continual training*—This step ensures that people share a common context for understanding their particular job and others' jobs. Communication between employees makes better sense when it's based on shared context.

- *Decision-making responsibilities compatible with job functions and knowledge*—The people who know the job best, because they do it, often have the responsibility for making decisions that come out of that job function because there is no time for having a decision come down through the organizational structure. The person lowest in the hierarchy can control the operations of the organization in some situations.

- *Open lines of communication between levels of the organization*—The easy flow of information comes from a system that dissolves rank and levels of authority that might otherwise inhibit people from openly talking to one another.

- *Redundant personnel in critical areas*—This system recognizes that people can misunderstand and be misunderstood. It reduces the risk of operational failure based on miscommunication and mistaken action by providing multiple sources of talk and action.

- *Backup communication systems*—If one system fails, another can do its job. The backup systems may be the same, or they may differ from each other so they can provide the same information in a different way.

- *Specialized language*—A specialized system of language gives people a way of talking to each other in shorthand, using terms that are only used by people in a specific organizational context they all share.

- *Personal accountability and responsibility within operational areas*—Everyone knows that they share the responsibility for the organization functioning without mistakes. Under this system, if you work for this organization, you must accept responsibility for your work within it. It's your responsibility to understand and be understood.

Training and organizational policies create and reinforce each aspect of this system. As an example, look at how one large and complex organization puts them into practice. The nuclear-powered aircraft carrier, USS *Enterprise*, employs six thousand people, has more than two thousand telephones, is twenty-four stories high, and has sufficient nuclear fuel to keep its engines running for fifteen years. It uses a variety of communication systems to ensure operational reliability, a point made all the more critical after a tragedy on board.

In 1969, a deck fire on board the *Enterprise* took its toll. An engine start-up unit's hot exhaust pipe ignited a missile, which hit an aircraft on the other side of the ship. The resulting chain reaction ended with five-hundred-pound bombs exploding on the flight deck. Nearly a hundred people died. The ship stayed in port for many weeks of repairs. The accident took a terrible toll in lives and time out of service. The work of the crew in preventing further loss of life during and after this tragic accident relied on clear communication with everyone understanding their roles and procedures.

As an organization, an aircraft carrier has many discrete and overlapping goals, including day and night flight operation needs, training needs, battle exercise needs, supply and service needs, navigational needs and personnel needs. Above all, the carrier needs to operate so that those responsible for carrying out the many different operations in a coordinated way understand each other at all times. Flight deck personnel call it "organized chaos." They each know their job but never know what will happen next. Misunderstanding at any time can lead to catastrophe.

Karlene Roberts has described the many systems the carrier uses to ensure clear communication. The ship has both direct and indirect information sources. The control tower, with responsibility for all flight and hangar deck operations, has over twenty different communication devices, including radios and sound-powered phones. The landing signal officer on the flight deck and his commander, the airboss in the control tower, can communicate with each other by telephone, a sound-activated "hotline," radio, a public address system, and a system that the tower can use to close down all flight operations.

Safe and efficient flight operations are at the core of the carrier's operational goals. These operations depend on everyone knowing their jobs and on everyone communicating clearly. The air tower talks with the navigational bridge to ensure a minimum wind of sixteen knots over the landing deck. The pilot of an F/A-18 fighter/attack aircraft on its final approach to the carrier talks to the airboss in the tower. The plane carries six Phoenix and

Sidewinder air-to-air missiles. The air traffic control center guides the final approach and tells the pilot to report when he sees the device that he uses to adjust his guide slope. The landing signal officer then takes control of the landing, gives the pilot advice, and keeps the aircraft within the landing parameters. The pilot reports the weight of his fuel load.

Using binoculars, the spotter identifies the type of approaching aircraft and calls out the weight setting for the arresting gear used to stop the plane on the 1,092-foot-long flight deck; checks and calls out the status of the landing gear; calls out the status of the deck (foul or clear); and finally calls out that the aircraft has landed, was waved off, or tried and failed in a landing attempt.

In this system, information on the approaching aircraft goes to the airboss from many different sources. This redundancy helps compensate for the tight time coupling of the many operations performed in landing an aircraft. If three people are looking at the same event and all three report the situation as the same, that makes up for the tight time frame in which the observations are made and reported. It explicitly creates shared context.

Superior Organizational Communication Creates Value

Even if lives aren't at stake in your company's operations, you can benefit from using some of the techniques employed by HROs. Systems that ensure clear communication increase operational efficiency and thus create value for the organization. Better operational procedures and processes can be built upon the base provided by these systems. A result may be a better product, whether it's a tangible good, service, system, or idea. Another may be better relationships within the organization and between the organization and its customers, clients, and anyone else in some relationship to it.

In order to decide how HRO systems can benefit your organization, you need to look at what your organization does, how it does it, who does it, and for whom. If you want to improve clear communication in your organization, you need to get people talking to each other with understanding. To do this, you have to know who shares a context with whom, and you have to use strategic talk to create that shared context where it doesn't exist.

Determining Communication Priorities

A range of organizations—from HROs, in which any operational misunderstanding can result in a major disaster, to the simplest and smallest retail operation, in which misunderstanding can result in dissatisfied customers—have a need for clear communication. Every organization needs to know how its different departments talk to one another. These units may vary from one organization to the next. However, in general terms they include finance, production, inventory, marketing, sales, taking and placing orders, scheduling, safety, delivery, employee and customer relations, quality control, and contracts. In small organizations (a hot dog stand, for instance), one person may perform the tasks inherent in all of these departments. However, in more complicated companies, these functions may be accomplished by many different people talking to each other and needing to make sense.

The following story shows what happens when an important operational area in a large financial organization needs clear communication but doesn't have the right system to deliver it. Imagine going to a local store to buy some blue jeans. The sales clerk slides your credit card through the scanner, but it doesn't accept the card. You think there's been some mistake, so when she suggests that she call the card company, you say, "Please do!" Suddenly, the clerk is taking out a pair of scissors to cut the card in half. You ask to speak to the card company representative on the phone. He says to tell the clerk not to cut the card. He's checking the problem. After a considerable time, he tells you that there's been an unfortunate mistake. One of your children has had his own card canceled and the computer automatically canceled all the accounts on which he was named, including yours—despite the fact that your son was actually no longer named on your account. There was nothing the representative could do to fix the problem just now. By then the store manager was involved and everyone was looking at you as though you had tried to steal the jeans.

This happened to me one Friday afternoon. It took until the following Wednesday to reinstate my card. In the meantime I used a different card. The original card company lost my business, goodwill, and any loyalty I might have felt. The problem arose because the company's system gave the power to cancel credit cards to machines instead of restricting it to human beings. Machines were talking to machines, when people should have been talking to people. It seems apparent that credit card companies should give customer relations high priority and have systems to maximize clear communication between customer and company. They should not allow machines to make important decisions that personally affect customers; such decisions should be made by real people. Misunderstandings with customers can do irreparable damage.

Conducting an inventory of organizational goals, structures, personnel, and operations can help illuminate the areas in which misunderstanding creates problems. The checklist presented in Exhibit 7.1 can help you examine your organization and its need for clear communication. You might want to go through this list and answer the questions for your own organization. You can use the list to identify areas in which communication must be clear and correctly understood so that tasks are done right the first time.

You'll notice that many of the organizational areas inventoried in the checklist are directly concerned with finances. This is no coincidence, for misunderstanding of the meaning of financial transactions can spell disaster for any organization. Finances must be a high-reliability area, and communication about money must be clear.

As you make use of the checklist, take a closer look at problems of misunderstanding within and across the areas in question. If there are problems, then implementing some communication systems used by HROs can help minimize or prevent them. Using this inventory will help show you where misunderstanding would do the greatest harm and where you might need to implement these

**Exhibit 7.1. Inventory of areas demanding clear
communication within organizations**

Which areas of your organization:

1. Have many different operational components, systems, or
   levels, and with specific or unique operating procedures,
   training routines, and operational hierarchies?
   Finance ___, production ___, inventory ___, marketing ___,
   sales ___, taking and placing orders ___, scheduling ___,
   safety ___, delivery ___, employee and customer relations ___,
   quality control ___, and contracts ___.

2. Have operations that cross many units and levels, with time-
   dependent processes and ordered sequences of operations that
   must be followed in order to reach a goal?
   Finance ___, production ___, inventory ___, marketing ___,
   sales ___, taking and placing orders ___, scheduling ___,
   safety ___, delivery ___, employee and customer relations ___,
   quality control ___, and contracts ___.

3. Have operations based on multiple levels, each with its own
   controls and regulating mechanisms?
   Finance ___, production ___, inventory ___, marketing ___,
   sales ___, taking and placing orders ___, scheduling ___,
   safety ___, delivery ___, employee and customer relations ___,
   quality control ___, and contracts ___.

4. Have operations characterized by large numbers of decision
   makers in the same and different areas?
   Finance ___, production ___, inventory ___, marketing ___,
   sales ___, taking and placing orders ___, scheduling ___,
   safety ___, delivery ___, employee and customer relations ___,
   quality control ___, and contracts ___.

5. Require high levels of accountability?
   Finance ___, production ___, inventory ___, marketing ___,
   sales ___, taking and placing orders ___, scheduling ___,
   safety ___, delivery ___, employee and customer relations ___,
   quality control ___, and contracts ___.

6. Require immediate feedback about decisions?
Finance ___, production ___, inventory ___, marketing ___,
sales ___, taking and placing orders ___, scheduling ___,
safety ___, delivery ___, employee and customer relations ___,
quality control ___, and contracts ___.

7. Have real-time activities that must happen quickly and in
sequence?
Finance ___, production ___, inventory ___, marketing ___,
sales ___, taking and placing orders ___, scheduling ___,
safety ___, delivery ___, employee and customer relations ___,
quality control ___, and contracts ___.

8. Have critical activities that must happen simultaneously
with no possibility of withdrawing or modifying operational
decisions once these activities have been started?
Finance ___, production ___, inventory ___, marketing ___,
sales ___, taking and placing orders ___, scheduling ___,
safety ___, delivery ___, employee and customer relations ___,
quality control ___, and contracts ___.

9. Have communication mainly with people outside the
organization?
Finance ___, production ___, inventory ___, marketing ___,
sales ___, taking and placing orders ___, scheduling ___,
safety ___, delivery ___, employee and customer relations ___,
quality control ___, and contracts ___.

What systems are in place for each of the areas you've checked off
for each question?

___ Continual training

___ Decision-making responsibilities compatible with job
functions and knowledge

___ Open lines of communication

___ Redundant personnel

___ Backup communication systems

___ Specialized language

___ Personal accountability and responsibility

systems along with increased use of strategic talk. You can be sure that these are areas in which people have to do more, not less, talking to each other.

Clarifying Agreements and Terminology

Transit Financial Holdings Inc. owned two insurance businesses. As Dan Westell reported, York Fire & Casualty Insurance Company, the first of these businesses, entered into an agreement with a reinsurance company. During the following year's audit, the vice president of the holding company learned of clauses in the agreement that appeared to have been misinterpreted by the holding company's insurance company. The vice president felt the company had no choice but to cancel the reinsurance agreement retroactive to its inception the year before.

As a result of this cancellation, claims and costs for that year went up and seriously affected the balance sheet for that and the following year. The initial reported loss for that fiscal year went from $1.5 million or $0.60 a share, to a loss of $3.8 million or $1.56 a share. And for the subsequent year, what had been a $1.5 million or $0.66 a share profit for the first nine months became a profit of only $196,000 or $0.08 a share at year-end.

The vice president and secretary of Transit Financial Holdings commented that his company and the reinsurer had not been communicating clearly. "What they said and what we heard wasn't the same thing," he said.

And if that wasn't enough, the second insurance company, Transit Insurance Company, incorrectly booked an actuarial calculation "due to a misinterpretation of the definition of net claims." That error, found in the subsequent year's audit, caused a $1.8 million increase in claims reserves and expenses.

These insurance companies had very costly errors that were harmful to each company, the policy holders, the shareholders, and the companies' relationship with government regulatory agencies. In one instance, it appears that those involved didn't take the necessary steps to check understanding of the terms of an agreement and thus avoid these problems. Here are specific steps that should be taken for critical agreements:

Face-to-face talk—The principals involved in the agreement must meet face-to-face. In any kind of negotiation, there must be sufficient talk about the meaning of the terms of the agreement so that all definitions are agreed to out loud by the principals involved.

Examples—Agreements should be accompanied by attachments containing examples of situations covered by the terms of the agreement. These attachments should be initialed by all parties.

Questions—All questions concerning the terms of the agreement—and the answers given to those questions—should be appended to the agreement and initialed by all parties.

Recordings—Audiotape or videotape the meetings between the parties to the agreement. This will provide the best record for resolving any future disputes about the meaning of the terms.

In the instance of the actuarial miscalculation, the actuaries apparently misinterpreted the meaning of "net claims," a standardly defined insurance term. The net claims figure is critical: it tells us how much the insurer must pay out. As the vice president commented, "It's not so much the auditors, it's the actuaries who got confused. These kinds of things can happen."

Misinterpretation by those who should know better can be prevented using two systems found in HROs:

Redundant systems—Using redundant systems, in which more than one person is responsible for checking the same event, provides an excellent check on misunderstanding. Remember the example of the aircraft carrier: four different people observe and report on the status of each approaching plane.

Training—Constant training ensures that everyone involved shares a common stock of knowledge about critical operational procedures and definitions. Training offers new knowledge and skills. Equally important, it gives everyone a chance to clarify and compare existing knowledge and skills.

Misunderstandings and mistakes can and do happen. However, by looking carefully at our organizations and incorporating some of the communication structures used in HROs, we can help decrease their frequency and minimize their harmful effects.

Making Directions Mesh with Background Knowledge

As we've just seen, we can't rely on people interpreting even specialized terms in the same way. If that's the case, how can we hope to communicate with clarity? How can we place our assumptions on solid ground?

Many organizations depend on what people already know for the success of their products. In so doing they need some baseline of what people know. Imagine that you own a food products company and that your packaging contains recipes for consumers to use in their own homes. How much must the consumer already know in order to make sense of your recipes? How much knowledge can you safely assume the consumer has?

The reality is that it wouldn't be possible to complete most recipes without already knowing much that's not explained in them. For example, here is a recipe for chocolate chip cookies:

2/3 cup soft shortening (part butter)
1/2 tsp. soda
1/2 tsp. salt
1 tsp. vanilla
1/2 cup granulated sugar
1/2 cup brown sugar (packed)

1/2 cup chopped nuts
1 egg
1 pkg. (6 oz.) semi-sweet chocolate pieces
1 1/2 cups flour

Heat oven to 375° (quick moderate). Mix shortening, sugars, egg, and vanilla thoroughly. Measure flour by dip-level-pour method or by sifting. Blend dry ingredients; stir in. Mix in nuts and chocolate pieces. Drop rounded teaspoonfuls 2 inches apart onto ungreased baking sheet. Bake 8 to 10 minutes. Cool slightly before removing from baking sheet. Makes 4 to 5 dozen 2-inch cookies.

No novice to the kitchen could use even this simple recipe successfully by doing only what the recipe prescribes. The cook needs some background knowledge. For example, what does the instruction to heat the oven mean? You can't possibly make your instructions inclusive enough to explain how each type of oven that might be used is to be lit and preheated. You must assume the consumer knows that or can find out elsewhere. Similarly, you assume the consumer understands that the rounded teaspoonfuls are to be of the cookie batter and that the cookie sheet, with the teaspoonfuls of batter on board, is to be placed in the oven—even though these points aren't stated explicitly. To include every step and bit of knowledge required, your recipes would run on for pages and could not fit on the outside of the box.

All directions—whether for baking cookies or for using a spreadsheet—work in the same way. To use any of them successfully, we must already have extensive background knowledge. If we don't, then we have to create it by talking through the directions so that all the implicit details that we must attend to are made explicit. In other words, in this instance, we have to be taught to cook. We could argue that through trial and error we might eventually end up with something that looks and tastes like a cookie. But time, energy, and resources would be wasted in the process. Instead, we generally depend on what people already know or we teach them.

Think of all the work done in your organization on a trial-and-error basis instead of through teaching and training. Perhaps you first tried to use your office computer by just referring to the manual. You soon realized that these manuals are written by people who already know how to use computers and who take certain knowledge about how to use computers for granted. Maybe the manual writers left out exactly the information you needed to fix your mistakes or go on to the next step. Nine times out of ten the "help" file can't answer your questions because it can't understand your problem, and there is no way for you to tell it. You can't have a conversation with your computer—at least not yet. So you try and try and then take a break. If you're lucky, you find someone who already knows how to do what you want to do and you talk to that person about the problem you're having. The answer may be to press the return key twice or use the special effects command in the page setup file. The solution may be straightforward, but chances are you could have read the manual straight through and not found those instructions. Computer manuals and programs don't solve our problems because they don't understand us as we need to be understood. They don't share our context for meaning. We need a person who has actually faced the same problems.

Directions present the same problems as all language. They depend on people's prior knowledge for them to make sense. Directions are easy to understand when we already know how to do an activity; but until we do, they're not simple. We must make explicit all the steps we take for granted. To do so, we have to recall how much we had to learn in order to become competent at the tasks we are describing, whether it's how to use a computer, bake chocolate chip cookies, or drive a car. For us they are now second nature and as familiar and as easy to do as spelling our own name.

Talking to people who are already proficient at the task described is the best way to understand directions. We need to have a conversation with the experts so that we can clarify their meaning. This is one form of training.

Training Improves the Bottom Line

When we want to ensure that people share a context for understanding, we give them explicit training. Training gives them the background knowledge to understand operations and gives us a context for understanding directions for doing things in the future. Training provides the foundation of HRO communication systems. As one officer on the *Enterprise* is reported to have said, "Our fundamental responsibility is training. We're like a baseball team that never goes into season."

Why put such emphasis on training? Training creates a shared context for understanding your job and the people with whom you work. And that shared context becomes the basis for shared meaning and interpretation. People who have trained together or who have been through similar training programs have the same background knowledge for understanding what other people are talking about on and in the job.

Not only does training teach skills and attitudes, it provides the basis for understanding other people's talk about the organization. Training, coupled with experience, gives people in the organization common ground for understanding so that their interpretation of others' talk will match the intended interpretation. A good example of this shared understanding can be seen in the following remarks made to Karlene Roberts during her study of the aircraft carrier USS *Carl Vinson*. The speakers have been asked to describe the primary operational goals of the ship:

> "The primary goal is to get the planes off the pointy end of the ship and back down on the flat end without mishap."
> "When we're flying, we're doing the job of the ship."
> "We don't feel good about the organization when we're in port. That's make work. We do the job of the ship when we're at sea."
> "This is just a bird farm. The birds come in, they get fed, and they go."

Training creates a shared culture, a community in which members share context for understanding. It makes the operational goals the priority for everyone.

Summary

High-reliability organizations have created systems to ensure operational reliability, including continual training, decision-making responsibilities compatible with job functions and knowledge, open lines of communication, redundant personnel, backup communication systems, specialized language, and personal accountability and responsibility. These systems aren't foolproof. Misunderstandings still occur; accidents still happen. And implementing the systems can be expensive. Nevertheless, many organizations seem willing to incur the expense because it pays off in the long run. Using these systems together with strategic talk can work effectively to prevent misunderstanding and ensure reliability. Organizations can gain a competitive advantage. Doing work right the first time creates efficient production, outstanding quality, and excellent service. These qualities lead to increased market share, better customer relations, and significant savings. If you reduce misunderstanding, you can end up saving more than you spend.

Although important, HRO systems by themselves aren't enough. Clear communication depends on the quality of the talk that takes place in the organization. Combining the structures used by HROs with strategic talk can help ensure that shared context for understanding is created.

Chapter Eight

Creating a New Accountability

If we go back and consider once more the meaning of the indexical and reflexive nature of language, we might be struck by the fact that we ever manage to make sense of each other at all. Indexicality tells us that context gives meaning to our talk, and reflexivity tells us that we're responsible for creating the context. We know that we use words to describe the world, including the world inside our heads, but the relationship between the words and the world is complex. Words can have many meanings, and so can the matter and events in the world. The world and the words we use to talk about it have a reflexive relationship. The world creates the words, and the words create the world.

We Are Accountable for Our Own Understanding

When we talk, we take the thoughts from our mind and make them available to others. We talk about our jobs and associates, our plans and goals, our problems and solutions. Even though jobs and people exist as movement in space or as physical objects, we create their meaning to us when we talk about them. Our plans and goals don't have any existence aside from our talk about them. Most of us don't think about that concept when we're talking to someone. Nevertheless, when we have a conversation with someone, we do jointly create a world in which having that conversation is possible.

Our role in creating this world is staggering and mundane at the same time. It's staggering because it puts a great deal of responsibility on our shoulders. Our world exists as we make sense of it. The meaning of what we say—or what anybody else says—can come only from our interpretation of it. It's our responsibility and nobody else's. This meaning comes from everything we think appropriate.

It's mundane because making sense of our world is our ordinary, everyday job. There is no time out from the responsibility to interpret the meaning of life as it comes at us in each moment of our existence. Whatever resources we may use in this interpretive process, the work of understanding life is our own. The understanding is also our own. Sometimes we appear to share this understanding with others and sometimes we don't. Shared understanding lets us live in a special relationship with others. Our lives would be impossible without some shared understanding. Indeed, people who don't share an understanding with others are often considered insane.

An organization's existence depends on people sharing an understanding of some of the ends and means of life in that organization. Life in a corporation, for example, involves some sharing of goals, purposes, processes, methods, places, times, names, relationships, and needs. Not everyone needs to share the same understanding of each of these with everyone else, but there has to be some overlap and sharing similar to the family resemblances discussed in Chapter Five. Shared understanding makes it possible for people in an organization to do their jobs as they should be done. Without shared understanding, the organization would be in chaos.

Given the indexical and reflexive nature of language, how is it that our organization (much less our world) is not complete chaos? If words are vague and ambiguous, how do we ever understand each other's talk? We understand it through work and trust. We work at interpreting what others say and they trust us to do that work. Sometimes we do it well and sometime we do it badly. Sometimes we care about doing it and sometimes we don't care at all. Sometimes we do it right and sometimes we do it wrong. Sometimes it matters and sometimes it doesn't. Whether or not we choose to use them, there are methods that can help us create shared understanding. Once we know what they are, we're accountable for shared understanding in a way we've never been before. When we understand misunderstanding and know how to use strategic talk to prevent it, *we are accountable for our own understanding.* How can we translate this knowledge into action that can transform our organizations?

From the Top Down

Top levels of the organization can use and advocate use of strategic talk as one aspect of leadership. An organization that wants to put the ideas from this book into practice can best do it from the top down. Once everyone in the organization knows that communication is to be top priority and learns the techniques of strategic talk, misunderstanding can no longer be used as an excuse for doing a job wrong. Knowing the importance of talk creates accountability.

Senior managers can help turn misunderstanding into understanding by teaching everyone in their organizations the reasons for misunderstanding, how to anticipate it, how to fix it and by setting an example in using strategic talk. Senior executives must show their managers that they're open to questions of clarification. Managers must do the same for their people, and so on throughout the organization.

When management wants to provide vision and leadership, they share their ideas with their employees. But they must use two-way communication to ensure that they're understood. When they want to empower their employees, they can give employees more say and control in organizational decisions. Many of the recent moves in organizational change (team-oriented approaches, knowledge-based companies, reduced management layers, the total quality movement, and coaching, for example) open up the organization to people sharing their understanding.

As one example, Thomas Stewart reports that General Electric's CEO, John F. Welch, Jr., introduced new techniques to increase productivity. Two of these, Work-Out and Best Practices, bring people together to talk through their problems and compare notes on *how* business get done rather than *what* gets done. They provide the opportunity for shared understanding in ways not possible before.

According to Bonnie Gordon, owners and managers of businesses said in interviews that they created special communication policies and structures to prevent employee conflicts from becoming major problems. These ranged from having a policy in which managers take their breaks with their employees, talking and listening to conversation, to family-type structures within the organization that create an atmosphere of trust, to emphasizing that employees are valued members. Some companies have used open-door policies to ensure that employees can talk to someone in a position of authority about work and personal problems. Above all, the emphasis is on being able to talk about problems, conflicts, and complaints out loud with someone who will try not to judge but to understand.

It's important that everyone understand why colleagues might say to them, "I'm sorry, but I'm not really clear on what you want. Could you make it a little clearer?" People need to feel free to say that without fear or guilt. In Chapter Seven we saw that one of the reasons for the success of HROs was the open lines of communication incorporated into their organizational structure. The top of the organizational pyramid needs to be accountable for clear communication in the same way as every other level. This top-down imposition of policies and structures strives to foster open communication about issues and details important to individuals in the organizations. In benefiting the employees, it benefits the organization as well.

From the Bottom Up and the Middle Out

In some organizations upper levels of management may not be willing to take an active role in advocating the use of strategic talk. Even in such organizations, there are ways to use formulations, questions and answers, paraphrases, examples, and stories without ruffling feathers or seeming slow. We can use strategic talk to get people to say more than they ordinarily would.

The key is to formulate the issues, perhaps by saying, for example, "Maria, I want to be sure that I understand exactly what you're saying." Then we can ask specific questions:

> "Who precisely do you want me to involve in this project?"
> "Can you give me a specific spending limit?"
> "What's the outside date that you need this?"
> "Will you make sure to tell me if anything changes that will affect this work?"

We can paraphrase:

> "Let me make sure I have this straight. I can use Ray and Louise to help me with this and you want us to give it first priority. You want some budget projections, but our outside limit is sixty-nine thousand. We have six weeks to get it done from the date you approve the budget. And you and I will meet on this each Friday afternoon to compare notes. Great. I'll get on it right away."

We can use examples:

> "Todd did an excellent job on a project similar to this one last year. Would you agree that I could use his work as a model?"

We can tell stories:

> "When I worked for our competition, my manager gave me a project to do which was a bit like this. Let me tell you what I did and see if you like the ideas I came up with."

Using strategic talk in this way helps us sound like the people we are: involved and involving, concerned and active. But even all these efforts can't ensure that people won't misunderstand each

other any more or that all conflicts can be solved to everyone's satisfaction. Some people will still think that they always make themselves clear and any misunderstanding is the other person's fault.
Hidden agendas will still be played out. Some people in your
organization may not want you to understand. They may give you
misinformation. They may unconsciously or intentionally deceive
you so that you will make mistakes while they shine in a glow of
competence and efficiency. Personalities will get in the way. If
you're shy, if you're insecure, if you're introverted, you may find it
more difficult to use strategic talk. But practice will help you overcome these problems.

In Difficult Situations

In addition to overcoming resistance to using strategic talk, how
can we avoid misunderstanding in situations when we have unpleasant or disappointing information to relate to people above us
in the organization? This is hard and dangerous to do in every organization. One approach to doing it is to imagine what you would
say and how you would say it if you worked in a family business but
you weren't family. For instance, how would you give your boss the
news that a member of his family is damaging the business? You
might begin by thinking about the risks and whether they're worth
it. In calculating the risks, you must realize that no one can ever
really know how someone will react to bad news since that reaction will depend on the context in which it's understood.

Here's an example of using strategic talk in such a situation.
Kevin was a manager in a family-run business, but he wasn't one of
the family. He discovered that Joseph, the boss's son, who was
involved in customer relations, had a drinking problem. He'd show
up late for meetings with customers, show up drunk, or not show
up at all. Kevin had to tell his boss that the reason for a drop in
sales and increased customer problems was his son's fault. How can
Kevin make sure that he's understood the way he wants to be?

How Kevin chooses to talk about this will depend on his personal style, his knowledge of the whole context including the per-

sonalities involved, the relationships within and outside the organization, and whatever else he thinks pertains to doing this unpleasant job. Above all, Kevin wants to be heard as having the company's best interests at heart. Knowing that he can't control his boss's reactions, Kevin can use his own talk to make his boss share his context for understanding.

In this kind of situation the history of the talking relationship between Kevin and his boss can be crucial. Remember that shared context is the most important element in understanding. If they have a good talking relationship—that is, if they use strategic talk regularly to share their ideas, concerns, problems, and solutions— then talking and understanding will be that much easier.

Kevin can formulate the talk by saying, "Harry, I've got some important feedback for you on the latest sales figures. I think I've found the problem. You're not going to like it, but the picture is pretty clear what's causing our customers to cancel their orders." This formulation explicitly says to hear what's about to be said as trouble talk. It places it in the context of the company's business rather than in the area of personalities or personal relationships. Most importantly, it draws upon the talking relationship that Kevin and Harry already have.

Having done this, Kevin can get into the details using business facts rather than personal judgments. First, he can give examples of specific instances in which customers have named Joseph as the reason for canceling orders. Second, Kevin can tell stories that explicitly detail the problems that Joseph has created. Third, Kevin can use examples and stories to show what he has tried to do with Joseph to solve the problem and why these attempts have not worked. Having done all this, Kevin can let Harry ask questions to clarify all that he has said. Kevin is using the talk to reflexively describe the problem and its cause and to create the context in which Harry can understand it.

Kevin's job was made easier because he had a good talking relationship with Harry. If the only time you talk to people is to bring them bad news, they won't be happy to see you. Think of how much you like talking to lawyers, dentists, doctors, and police officers.

Prepare for situations in which you will have to relate bad news by establishing good talking relationships. It's easier to relate to people you talk to on a regular basis than to people to whom you rarely talk. Knowing people's talk means knowing them. It provides a good context for understanding the message, good or bad.

Communication Outside the Organization

Even more important than bottom-up and middle-out communication is communication with the organization's customers. We think of customers expressing themselves with their dollars or in market research. Now many organizations are trying their best to get feedback from their clients and customers on their service or product. If you have recently flown on an airline, stayed in a hotel, or bought a new car, you know that it's difficult to avoid customer satisfaction questionnaires and surveys.

A company in Japan has taken customer-company communication a step further. It builds bicycles to the individual customer's measurements on its assembly line for only 10 percent more than the regular price. The company can create 11,231,862 different models using this system.

The firm's efforts point to increasing recognition of the power of open communication for serving the marketplace in the best and most efficient possible way. True customer satisfaction begins when, within some practical limits, the customer designs the product. Advances in computers and telecommunications give us the technology to do the job, and new communication policies and structures within the organization allow the customers to make their wishes known. If strategic talk is properly used, customers' wishes can then be properly understood. This, then, is the ideal. How do we get there?

Steps to Take

What can you, as an individual, do to change your organization from one that suffers from the normal amount of misunderstanding and all the costs associated with that, to one that controls misunderstanding? There are a number of steps to take, including understanding the indexicality and reflexivity of language, requiring communication, and taking turns at talk.

Understand the Indexicality and Reflexivity of Language

Teaching people that language is indexical and reflexive is a good beginning in decreasing misunderstanding. The two concepts of indexicality and reflexivity are the key to understanding the equivocal and contingent nature of communication. Understanding indexicality is fairly easy for most people; understanding reflexivity is not.

The major problem in understanding reflexivity seems to be the circular and somewhat paradoxical relationship involved. People find it hard to fully comprehend the idea of a world that creates and is created by language. However, with persistence and lots of practical examples, people do ultimately begin to get the idea that they're actively and jointly involved with others in creating the world by drawing upon the world that has created them.

Understanding indexicality and reflexivity gives people power, the power to know how and why they must talk differently when they really need to understand. Training people in this understanding gives them a shared context for clear communication in the organization. The best training exercises come from familiar, everyday situations. Those participating in training groups can contribute instances of misunderstanding that have affected their work in some way. We can use these instances to illustrate all the points of misunderstanding that come from the nature of language. They can be used to coach people in using strategic talk in important situations to avoid misunderstanding and ensure clear communication. There are no tricks or shortcuts. The bottom line is simply understanding how language works. Once we understand, we have the freedom and the responsibility to use language with care. Understanding language means knowing that talk is the best solution to the problem of misunderstanding.

Banish Mind Reading

Show people that the organization discourages an attitude that demands that people attempt to read others' minds. Make sure that important background information for understanding is made explicit. Everyone must be accountable for understanding and making themselves understood. Probing questions about points that might previously have seemed obvious to the speaker are now acceptable, and not using them is unacceptable. Everyone must feel obliged to make sure they understand the speaker—and the atmosphere must support the use of strategic talk.

It's not easy to accept probing questions unless you're really committed to clear communication. William Corsaro has studied what he calls "clarification requests." These are requests to make sure that we and the others understand what the others are saying. In using clarification requests, adults suspend use of the et cetera principle, under which, in normal talk, the listener is expected to fill in the details not explicitly stated by the speaker but that are needed to understand the talk.

In fact, adults use clarification requests significantly more with children than with other adults. In adult-child interactions, the adults will often respond by saying "what," "huh," and "hum"; repeating in a questioning way what the child has said; or repeating and expanding what the child has said. In contrast, adults talking to adults tend to use the et cetera principle. Adults expect other adults to fill in all the missing information, which is why most people are reluctant to go too far asking for clarification.

Here's a reminder of how we use the et cetera principle in a typical work situation. The unspoken background information each person is using to make sense of the talk is shown to the right of the spoken dialogue:

Elaine: Mark, ready for the meeting this morning?

[I might as well remind Mark of this morning's meeting. It's a very important one to discuss production schedules for the fall line. Mark's input will be useful

because he can give us some of the latest
figures on production costs. The meeting's at 10:30 in the boardroom and will
probably last through lunch.]

Mark: You bet.

[I wouldn't miss this meeting for the world.
At last we can have some serious discussion of some of the production problems
we're having. I think we better be prepared to face the possibility of moving our
factory south where production and labor
costs are lower. I wonder what we'll get
for lunch. It should be a long meeting.]

Elaine: Should
be interesting.

[Mark thinks we need new machines in
our factory. I don't see how we can possibly afford them in the current market. I
expect there'll be a fight over this.]

Mark: Do you
have the
latest figures?

[I know sales have been slower than budget projections. Elaine should be able to
give us the latest figures that will show
the only way we can compete in the
future is to reduce costs. I don't think
anyone can disagree.]

Elaine: They'll
be there.

[I wonder which figures he means? The last
quarter sales figures aren't in yet. But it
looks like they'll be very close to what
we budgeted and better than our latest
projections. We should consider subcontracting some of our production
offshore.]

Here's another version of the same conversation, but this time
with more explicit talk and less dependence on the other person
filling in the appropriate background information.

Elaine: Mark, I wanted to talk to you about this morning's meeting. The meeting's at 10:30 in the boardroom and will probably last through lunch.

It's important that we discuss the production schedules for the fall line. Do you have the latest figures on production costs?

[I'd better remind Mark of it since his input on production costs will be useful.]

Mark: You bet. I think there are some really important issues to discuss about the production end. I think we better be prepared to face the possibility of moving our factory south where production and labor costs are lower.

[I wouldn't miss this meeting for the world, but it could be a long one. I wonder what we'll get for lunch.]

Elaine: I thought you were going to fight for new machines in our factory. But we can't afford them right now. I think there's even a better solution to the problem than moving the whole operation.

[I hope Mark understands that I'm not trying to upstage him with this idea.]

Mark: I'd like to hear what you think it is. But first, do you have the latest sales figures? I heard from Phil that they're five percent below budget projections. It seems to me that the only way we can compete in the future is to reduce costs. Do you agree?

[If the figures are really that low then we've got to act in a hurry. The best way is to cut our labor costs. Wage rates in the south are considerably lower just now.]

Elaine: The last quarter sales figures aren't in yet. But it looks like they'll be very close to what we budgeted and better than our latest projections. In any case, I think you're right. We still have to reduce costs. Have you considered subcontracting some of our production offshore?

[I can't see us purchasing a new production facility just to cut labor costs.]

Mark: I've done some looking into it. In fact one of our competitors has been doing it for the past three years. Their production manager happens to be a personal friend of mine and I have some horror stories from him about quality control, local taxation problems, and downtime for the machinery.

[I'd better call Joe before the meeting to confirm those stories.]

I know it's cheaper on paper, but it might turn out to be more expensive in fact. Do you have any success stories you can tell me?

Elaine: No, I haven't heard anything one way or the other. I'm just looking for a way to improve our bottom line. I know that's also your main concern.

[If we could find some reliable jobber offshore who could guarantee supplying on time, that would be so much cheaper and simpler than buying equipment ourselves. And conditions change so quickly these days.]

If you're to make strides toward understanding, be ready to suspend use of the et cetera principle. There will always be thoughts you don't express, but you can still make many more of your thoughts explicit. It's easier to do this when your listeners understand what you're doing. Otherwise, people may wonder why you're asking so many questions or why you don't know the answer already. We're all so used to filling in meaning for others and expecting others to do the same for us that we have to get used to trying to make talk more explicit.

Making sure that we understand each other clearly and precisely requires more talk than normal. For example, we can formulate what we're about to do by saying, "Look, it's really important that I understand precisely what you're saying. I think I might not have all of the background information I need to do that. So would you mind if I asked you some really important questions for clarification?" Doing this lets the other person put our words in the right context.

We can do the same thing in any other situation where we think our attempt at clarifying might be thought unusual. Even with people who know and accept how vague and ambiguous language is, it never hurts to remind them by using a formulation, such as "We both know the problems with understanding what people mean. So tell me if I've got this right."

Take Turns at Talk

We make sense of each other by taking turns as speaker and listener. Through the give-and-take of talk we have the opportunity to make sense of each other. One-way communication may not be understood at all; we have to have some kind of feedback to check for understanding. People have to talk or act in response to our talk for us to know that they understood us or even heard us. Unless the talk requires people to act (such as having the budget figures on your desk by noon) or talk (such as asking your associate what she knows about a prospective client), we can't know what others heard. We can each use our turn to make our understanding more explicit.

Using Strategic Talk

We work together. We build houses and computers and cellular phones. We make pies and dresses and furniture polish. We create music and junk bonds and statues. We invent aspirin and mouse-traps and excuses. We discover oil and microwaves and quasars. We perform operas and medical examinations and our duty. We interpret laws and rules and foreign languages. All is not chaos. We have a reasonably successful social world in which we complete tasks with others. We seem to share enough understanding to do this. However, we also misunderstand each other. Some tasks get done wrong or not at all. The same language that enables us to work together successfully can also prevent us from doing so.

The job of this book has been to suggest how we can use language to maximize shared understanding so that we can work better together. When we begin consciously and deliberately to formulate our talk, to ask questions and give answers, to put other's talk into our own words, to use examples to make what we're saying concrete, and to tell stories to illustrate what we mean, we've gone as far as human beings can go to use talk to prevent misunderstanding. In order to do this, we have to see that indexicality and reflexivity are fundamental features of language and that they will never go away. Once we see and understand this, we're in a better position to use our ordinary language to ensure that we can create shared context.

Context can be huge and complicated or small and simple. Either way, it's the basis for understanding. To create shared context we make the ideas in our mind explicit in our talk. To do this we use ordinary forms of talk called formulations, questions and answers, paraphrasing, examples, and stories. These are not precise or technical categories of talk. They exist as they function to make our thoughts explicit in our talk so they're available for others to use, either as a topic for further talk or as a resource for understanding what we've said.

Here's a practical example. Dylan runs a small auto repair shop and is repairing a 1984 Buick, planning to have it ready for the customer in two days. Unfortunately, the auto parts store sold him the wrong part and thus set him back. Since this is not the first time he has received the wrong part, Dylan has come up with a theory: the parts people don't ask the right questions when he orders the parts, and they don't understand or read the parts manuals well enough. This, together with the fact that Dylan has not actively confirmed the specifications, can explain why his requests are so often filled incorrectly.

His conversation with the parts department clerk had gone like this:

> *Parts:* What can I do for you?
>
> *Dylan:* I need a right front axle boot for a 1984 Buick Century Special Edition.
>
> *Parts:* Okay. I'll get it for you.

Back at Dylan's shop, the part did not fit. Ideally, the conversation needed to go more like the following:

> *Parts:* What can I do for you?
>
> *Dylan:* I need a front right axle boot for a 1984 Buick Century Special Edition.
>
> *Parts:* That's a front right axle boot for a 1984 Buick Century Special Edition?
>
> *Dylan:* Yes.
>
> *Parts:* We should have one of those. I'll look it up. . . . That's the Special Edition?
>
> *Dylan:* Yes. The one with the heavy-duty front end.
>
> *Parts:* It has a heavy-duty front end?
>
> *Dylan:* Yes. Here's the part specs from the manual.
>
> *Parts:* Good. Here's the right one. It's thicker than the ordinary boot. Let's check the specs to make sure.
>
> *Dylan:* Thanks.

If Dylan and the clerk had made their thoughts and knowledge explicit, the original misunderstanding might have been avoided.

If the clerk in parts hadn't volunteered to check the specs, as he did the second time around, Dylan should have requested that he do so.

Misunderstandings for most of us are a daily occurrence. The more complicated our lives, the more likely we will waste time and money trying to undo the damage caused by misunderstanding. Just think how often you spend time trying to remedy misunderstandings—minor or major—with your bank, your suppliers, or your customers.

Laura, chief financial officer for a public company, had to spend half the day on the phone when people in the bank and the brokerage company misunderstood her instructions regarding registration of a new corporate bond issue her company received. New forms had to be filled in and many telephone calls made. The brokerage back office had registered the bonds in the wrong name and delivered the wrong number of bonds to the bank. More phone calls to the bank and the broker were made. The broker had to pick up the bonds, return them to the transfer agent, and have them reissued.

As if these misunderstandings weren't enough, the next day Laura discovered that her corporate travel agent booked her business flight to the West Coast on the wrong day and had already issued the ticket. Company policy required using advance purchase fares whenever possible to save money. But this kind of ticket permitted no changes. She called the agent. The agent had to call the airline and get special permission to change the ticket. The agent then had to return the incorrect ticket, and a new ticket was issued and delivered by courier to Laura's office.

Were these mistakes caused by incompetence or misunderstanding? We may never know the "real" cause. However, strategic talk can help you spend less time undoing mistakes caused by misunderstandings. Knowing the importance of strategic talk to individuals and organizations, how can we make it happen?

Summary: Making Strategic Talk the Norm

It goes without saying that if we don't listen to what people are saying, we can't hope to understand them. Listening is a cornerstone of clear communication. In fact, "power listening" was one of the catch phrases of the eighties. Communications consultants taught that effective listening could help improve productivity, sales, morale, and the general efficiency of the organization. These are all valid points, as far as they go.

The message of this book takes listening for granted. That doesn't mean that we should take listening for granted. Just the opposite; in fact, we all need to work at improving our listening skills and habits. However, even if we listen as carefully as possible, even if we hear every nuance of a person's words, we still can't assume that we understand what people are saying in the same way they intend us to understand them.

As Tom Harris reported, Germaine Knapp, president of Words-mart Inc., has some succinct words on the topic. She has said, "Never end a conversation without being sure what was said—and why. Furthermore, don't pretend you understand when you don't. Chances are the speaker, not you, caused the confusion. So don't walk away and later make mistakes that you, not the speaker, will be held responsible for."

It's up to us, as the listeners, to clear up any potential misunderstanding. We must remember that the speaker already knows what he or she means. Good listening skills are only half the solution. The other half is good talking skills using strategic talk.

Knowing why strategic talk is necessary makes us all accountable. With this knowledge, we can't claim that we don't understand and use that as an excuse for not doing a critical job right the first time. Instead, we must start to use this knowledge. We must begin, even in small ways, to use strategic talk in our organizations. As misunderstandings decrease and efficiency and understanding increase, we will rely on strategic talk more frequently—and with ever more positive results. Soon we will see that the applications of these strategies are endless. Further, once we've made clear communication a major goal of our organization, we will recognize that there is no time out from working at making sense of each other. The job is never done. It must always be "Again, for the first time!"

Checklist Part Three

Acknowledge that in a business setting, where people's jobs and livelihoods are at stake and where power and control figure in prominently, using strategic talk can seem daunting.

Get commitment from those who have the power to open up the organization to free and easy communication. People will talk when they think they have nothing to fear from saying what is on their minds.

Use strategic talk to help others understand your vision as a leader.

Expect misunderstanding and help prevent it by creating an organization in which two-way and face-to-face communication is demanded at all levels.

Establish and maintain policies to create understanding:

- Open lines of communication.
- Allow people to express their own interpretation of what is said and written.
- Support strategic talk.
- Place the responsibility to recognize, fix, and communicate about problems, in employees' operational area.
- Ask real questions, consider employees' talk as a window on your operation, and reward people for talking about the organization with you.
- Create a specialized language for communication of critical information.
- Recognize that the overall communication structure of an organization is only as strong as the communication skills of each person in the organization.

Support understanding with continual training, mediated communication, inverted pyramid for clear communication, and backups.

Recognize that maintaining relationships is critical to clear communication.

Understand that people's practical interests will affect the way they understand what you are saying.

Identify and examine your own priorities for clear communication and learn how to support them.

Conduct an inventory of organizational goals, structures, personnel, and operations to illuminate the areas in which misunderstanding creates problems.

Share goals, purposes, processes, methods, places, times, names, relationships, and needs.

Acknowledge that we are each accountable for our own understanding.

Be understanding if a colleague says to you, "I'm sorry, but I'm not really clear on what you want. Could you make it a little clearer?" Encourage everyone in the organization to do the same.

Establish regular talking relationships with your associates to provide a context for understanding.

Know that if clear communication is a major goal of your organization, there is no time out from working at making sense of each other. The responsibility to interpret the meaning of talk exists in each moment.

References

"A Moment of Truth." *Newsweek*, Oct. 21, 1991, pp. 24, 34–37.

Associated Press. "Ex Athlete Seeking Justice: Olympic Women's Champion of 1930's May Have Been Man." *Globe and Mail*, Dec. 5, 1991, p. A14.

Austin, J. L. *How to Do Things with Words*. Oxford: Clarendon Press, 1962.

Corsaro, W. "The Clarification Request as a Feature of Adult Interactive Style with Young Children." *Language in Society*, 1978, 6, 183–207.

Farnham, A. "The Trust Gap." *Fortune*, Dec. 4, 1989, pp. 56–72.

Garfinkel, H. *Studies in Ethnomethodology*. Englewood Cliffs, N. J.: Prentice-Hall, 1967.

Garfinkel, H., and Sacks, H. "On Formal Structures of Practical Actions." In J. C. McKinney and E. A. Tiryakian (eds.), *Theoretical Sociology*. East Norwalk, Conn.: Appleton & Lange, 1970.

Gibb-Clark, M. "Making Mentors." *Globe and Mail*, July 3, 1990, Sec. B, p. 4.

Gordon, B. "Settling Conflicts Among Your Workers." *Nation's Business*, Mar. 1988, pp. 71–71.

Harris, T. "Listen Carefully." *Nation's Business*, June 1989, p. 78.

Henley, N., and Kramarae, C. "Gender, Power and Miscommunication." In N. Coupland, H. Giles, and J. M. Wiemann (eds.), *"Miscommunication" and Problematic Talk*. Newbury Park, Calif.: Sage, 1991.

Heritage, J. *Garfinkel and Ethnomethodology*. Cambridge: Polity Press, 1984.

Heyman, R. D. "Natural Language and Computer Conferencing." In S. Thomas (ed.), *Studies in Communication* (Vol. 4). Norwood, N.J.: Ablex, 1986.

Hull, T. "Argument Delayed Ambulance." *Dallas Times Herald*, Mar. 6, 1984, p. 1A.

Johnson, H. M. *Sociology: A Systematic Introduction*. London: Routledge & Kegan Paul, 1968.

Kaplan, D., McDaniel, A., and Anin, P. "Anatomy of a Debate." *Newsweek*, Oct. 21, 1991, pp. 26–34.

Karr, A. R. "Labor Letter: Special News Report on People and Their Jobs in Offices, Fields and Factories." *Wall Street Journal*, Jan. 30, 1990, Sec. A, p. 1.

Klass, P. J. "Predeparture Clearance to Be Sent via Data Link at Major Airports." *Aviation Week & Space Technology*, June 25, 1990, 132(26), 43, 46.

Knotts, R. "Cross-Cultural Management: Transformations and Adaptations." *Business Horizons*, 1989, 32(1), 29–33.

Lascher, Jr., E. L., and La Porte, T. R. "Lessons from a Reliability Crisis." *Public Utilities Fortnightly*, June 7, 1990, 125(12), 11–15.

Little, B. "The Heavy Metal Band." *Globe & Mail*, Sept. 1, 1992, p. B18.

Little, B. "Profit from Chaos." *Globe & Mail*, June 16, 1993, p. B20.

Peters, R. S. *Ethics and Education*. London: Allen & Unwin, 1968.

Presidential Commission on the Space Shuttle Challenger Accident. *Report of the Presidential Commission on the Space Shuttle Accident* (5 vols.). Washington, D.C.: General Printing Office, 1986.

Raymond, J. "Worth Repeating." *Globe & Mail*, Jan. 28, 1993, Sec. B, p. 6.

Rice, F. "Champions of Communication." *Fortune*, 1991, *124*(12), 201–204.

Roberts, K. "Some Characteristics of One Type of High Reliability Organization." *Organization Science*, 1990, *1*(2), 160–176.

Schneebaum, T. *Keep the River on Your Right.* New York: Grove Press, 1969.

Searle, J. *Speech Acts.* Cambridge: Cambridge University Press, 1969.

Solomon, J. "Workplace: As Cultural Diversity of Workers Grow, Experts Urge Appreciation of Differences." *Wall Street Journal*, Sept. 12, 1990, Sec. B, p. 1.

Stewart, T. "GE Keeps Those Ideas Coming." *Fortune*, Aug. 12, 1991, *124*(4), 40–49.

Suchman, L. A. *Plans and Situated Actions: The Problem of Human-Machine Communication.* Palo Alto, Calif.: Xerox, 1985.

Tannen, D. *You Just Don't Understand: Conversations Between Men and Women.* New York: Morrow, 1990.

"The Empowered Customer." *Globe & Mail*, Dec. 8, 1992, p. B18.

Tompkins, P. K. "Management Qua Communication in Rocket Research and Development." *Communication Monographs*, 1977, *44*, 1–26.

West, C., and Frankel, R. "Miscommunication in Medicine." In N. Coupland, H. Giles, and J. M. Wiemann (eds.), *"Miscommunication" and Problematic Talk.* Newbury Park, Calif.: Sage, 1991.

Westell, D. "Misinterpretations Hurt Transit." *Globe & Mail*, May 3, 1991, p. 4.

Whalen, J., Zimmerman, D., and Whalen, M. "When Words Fail: A Single Case Analysis." *Social Problems*, 1988, *35*(4), 335–361.

Williamson, R. "How Not to Deal with Japanese." *Globe & Mail*, Dec. 21, 1991, pp. B1, B4.

Winsor, D. "Communications Failures Contributing to the Challenger Accident: An Example for Technical Communicators." *IEEE Transactions on Professional Communication*, 1988, *31*(3), 101–107.

Wittgenstein, L. *Philosophical Investigations.* London: Basil Blackwell & Mott, 1953.

Index

A

Accountability: for customers, 162; of individual, 162–168; of lower/middle levels, 158–162; of management, 157–158; for understanding, 141, 155–157, 174; for using strategic talk, 171–172

Action: informed, 45; talking as, 65–70; using talk for, 52–57

Advertising agency, 59–60

Agreements, clarification of, 148–150

Air traffic controllers (ATCs), 88–89, 142–143

Aircraft carrier systems, 141–143, 153

Airline predeparture clearances (PDCs), 88–89

Akaramas tribe, 28

Ambiguity: of context, 10; of language, 8, 11, 22; of talk, 11–14, 35–36; of written communication, 73–76, 77

Andrews, J., 100

Anger, and strategic talk, 51

Anin, P., 102

Answers. *See* Questions and answers

Asian culture, 106–107

Associated Press, 100

Audience size, 91

Austin, J. L., 65

Awareness, in intercultural communication, 97–98

B

Background knowledge: assumption of, 164–165; providing of, 165–168; and providing directions, 150–152; and shared context, 28–30; training for, 153–154

Backup communication systems, 126, 141

Bottom-up communication, 126–127, 141, 158–162

Boys, 98–99

"Breaching" experiments, 12–13

Business meetings, 10

C

Challenger space shuttle disaster, 78–81, 139–140

Checklists, 48, 110, 173–174

Chief executive officers (CEOs): communication effectiveness of, 8, 121, 132–133; two-way talk with, 157–158

Children, talking of, 34

Clarification requests, 164

Commitment: and promises, 67–69; to strategic talk, 114–115, 134, 173

Communication: importance of, 8, 115–118; with individuals vs. social groups, 98, 103; inventory of areas needing, 146–147; organizational structures for, 125–127, 140–143, 158; policies for, 119–124, 140–143, 158; prioritizing, 144–148

Communicators, demand for, 8

"Company bible," 72–73

Computer conferencing, 87, 88

Conflict, avoidance of, 128–129, 158

Consumer research, 62–65, 110, 162

Context, 9, 22; consequences of unshared, 18–20; and consumer research, 63–65; deep differences in, 20–21; determining of, 15; framing of, 17–18, 25; indexicality of, 10; and job descriptions, 82–83; need for shared, 11, 17–18; and personal interests, 129–132; of promises, 68–69; for relating unpleasant news, 160–161; and speech acts, 66–67. *See also* Shared context

Contracts, written, 75–77

Control, and communication, 113–114

Conversation analysis, 8–11

Cooperation, and girls, 98

Correspondence, using talk to clarify, 77–81

Corsaro, W., 164

Credit card companies, 144–145

Crisis management, 132

Critical information, specialized language for, 124, 141. *See also* High-reliability organizations

Also Available from the
Jossey-Bass Business & Management Series